Sedona Soul Stretch

10 Ancient Yoga Principles to Heighten Consciousness and Performance

Johanna Mosca, Ph.D.

Published by Sedona Spirit Yoga

ISBN: 979-8-9885400-0-7 (Paperback)

ISBN: 979-8-9885400-1-4 (E-Book)

About Johanna Mosca, Ph.D.

Captivated by the mystical beauty of Sedona, Johanna Maheshvari Mosca left her long-time job as an educational consultant in NYC in 1992 and camped out in Sedona, AZ, for fourteen months. Johanna enjoyed practicing Yoga on the red rocks so much that she founded Sedona Spirit Yoga & Vortex Journeys, which has now won Best-of-Sedona Awards for seven consecutive years from 2019 to 2025. Johanna holds a Ph.D. from New York University and six Yoga and Meditation Certifications. She also earned two 300-hour program diplomas as a Master Practitioner of Richard Miller's i-Rest Meditation, Inner Restoration Yoga Nidra, and Alberto Villoldo's Four Winds Academy Shamanic Energy Medicine. Johanna has 33 years of experience teaching Yoga and pursuing advanced studies in Yoga and Meditation training.

In recent years, Johanna became fascinated with *PSYCH-K®* belief change and was certified as a *PSYCH-K®* Facilitator through Basic, Advanced, and Master *PSYCH-K® workshops*. She is the author of several books and CDs, including ***YogaLife: 10 Steps to Freedom*** and ***Teen Triumph: 10 Ways to a Winning Life***. Johanna's passion lies in guiding guests inward as she shares her lifelong study and practice of Yoga, Meditation, *PSYCH-K®*, and Shamanic Energy Clearing. To learn more about Johanna, visit johannamoscaphd.com.

Dedication

I dedicate ***Sedona Soul Stretch*** with love and blessings to my dear friend Christy Dantin, who is my supportive confidante and inspiring cheerleader. Christy is a delightful southern belle, brilliant business woman, and devoted mother, who telephones from Louisiana to visit daily, serving as my precious daughter, my loving sister, my surrogate mom, my gifted unpaid personal assistant, and my blessed angel. Christy, may you always thrive!

Acknowledgments

With heartfelt appreciation, I acknowledge my devoted friends and editors, Pesi Dinnerstein and Kat Drayton, who tirelessly offered their assistance with wording throughout the various stages of writing and rewriting. I also extend my thanks to the early readers, my dear friends Tina Mancusi, Christy Dantin, Debbie Cutler, and Anna Mannino, who were the first to embrace and support the ***Sedona Soul Stretch*** book. And, I express my deepest thanks to my mentor Richard Miller for writing such a brilliant foreword to introduce ***Sedona Soul Stretch***. Lastly, I hold in my heart all of the clients, students, and teachers who continue to help me transcend my human challenges and reach my highest consciousness.

Foreword by Richard C. Miller, Ph.D.

We live in a world where we can, at times, feel overrun with the divisiveness and conflicts that prevail within and around ourselves. When we do, we need reminders as to how we can tap into our innate light of intelligence that always knows the right responses we need to engage that enable us to feel in harmony both within and in the world around us. Here we tap into a truth that cannot be dimmed or extinguished—the light that resides within us, which always remains pristine no matter our circumstances. We just need to know how to bring it to our conscious awareness and embodied experience.

Many around the world engage in rituals to celebrate the light that resides within. Christians celebrate the luminous appearance of the Christ child, as an embodiment of love and redemption. Jews celebrate the holy miracle of the oil lamp that burned for eight days in the Temple. Buddhists commemorate Buddha's reminding them to become a light unto themselves. And Patañjali, in his Yoga Sutras, celebrates ten principles and practices for activating the light within to achieve inner peace and outer social harmony. And now, following Patañjali's lead, you have in your hands Johanna Mosca's marvelous book that shows you how to bring forward these ten principles, so that you, too, can tap into and celebrate the light of your own innate intelligence, and be a light unto yourself, and to those around you. There is an ancient saying from the Bṛhadāraṇyaka Upaniṣad: "Whenever we separate within or without with the 'what is of life' we will always find ourselves experiencing some form of stress, distress, anxiety, fear, or defensive reactivity."[1] And while it's natural for

[1] Miller, Richard. Unpublished manuscript of the Bṛhadāraṇyaka Upaniṣad.

us as human beings to become reactively caught up in our desire for change, Mosca's book highlights an alternative path through our embracing ten ancient principles that empower us with skillful means for navigating life's challenges successfully.

Buddha wisely noted that it is not the first arrow—our initial feeling of distress—that harms us. It is the second arrow, when we are anxious about being anxious, afraid of being afraid, angry about being angry, and defensive about being defensive, that inflicts damage.

Our job is to be sensitive to the first arrow, for it is the first arrow that points to where we're separating within ourselves. Here, at this source point of separation, we can rediscover our inner light and intelligence that guides us towards actions that restore our inner and outer peace and harmony. In the words of Rilke, "Ah, not to be cut off, not through the slightest partition shut out from the law of the stars. The *inner—intensified [light]—hurled through with birds and deep with the winds of homecoming."*[2]

Rilke knows that the instant we separate, we cut ourselves off from our inner light and intelligence. He rightfully knows that the feelings that arise when we separate—stress, distress, anxiety, fear, and defensiveness—are harbingers, sent by our body's innate intelligence to turn us back into ourselves, to the inner garden we each have been given to tend. Here, Rumi's words echo the charge given to us by life—to tend our own garden first—and by so doing, attain the ability to be a light unto ourselves. Only then, can we be a light unto others and the world around us.

"Our defects are the ways that glory gets manifested. Whosoever sees clearly what's diseased in himself begins to gallop on the way. Don't turn your head. Keep looking at the bandaged place. That's where the light enters you."[3]

It is with this understanding that Mosca also urges us to face our adversities through embracing the ten principles set out by Patāñjali, that enable us to rediscover, embrace, and embody our inner light, no matter our circumstance. Mosca takes up the wisdom given to us by the sage

[2] Mitchell, S. *Ahead of All Parting: The Selected Poetry and Prose of Rainer Maria Rilke.* 1995. Modern Library. NY, NY.

[3] Barks, Coleman. *The Essential Rumi.* 2004. Harper One, San Francisco, CA.

Patāñjali in his recognition that it's not possible to control external events. What he/she recommends instead is that we learn to control our mind so we can respond appropriately and harmoniously to both our inner and outer circumstances.

I've come to appreciate that we forget, as much as we remember, what it is that we are supposed to do. So, I deeply appreciate Mosca's elucidating these ten simple principles that we can all welcome into our lives. As stated by Kṣemarāja in his 4th century text, the Pratyabijñāhṛdayam, we are all born from a common essence that has given birth to everything—stars, planets, mountains, trees, animals, insects, and every human being. Since everything is an expression of this ineffable mysterious essence, then both forgetting and remembering are also movements of essence.

When we forget—when we have moments of anger or defensive reactivity—these, too, are expressions of, and pointers back to where we're separating from essence. With awe, wonder, and curiosity, we can then exclaim, *"Amazing! Look how essence is presenting herself in this moment—as anger and reactive defensiveness—as movements of forgetting and separation."*

We can, through incorporating these ten principles, learn, as Mosca points out, to meet our moments of separation with kindness, compassionate understanding, and love. We can meet them as messengers, with gratitude as Rumi also so rightly invites us to when he affirms that— *"The dark thought, the shame, the malice, meet them at the door laughing, and invite them in. Be grateful for whoever comes because each has been sent as a guide from beyond."*[4]

Our thoughts and feelings are not inherently good or bad. They just are. When we are heedfully vigilant, mindful, and attentive, we have the ability to nourish what is innate within ourselves that is mysterious, ineffable, benevolent, inherently compassionate, loving, kind, and intelligent.

In the face of adversity, heedful vigilance and curiosity are our safest courses of action. When we meet our moments of reactive distress, anxiety, fear, and defensiveness with the attitude of compassionate understanding, we discover a doorway back to love and connection with

[4] Barks, Coleman. *The Soul of Rumi.* 2001. HarperOne. San Francisco, CA.

ourselves and the world around us. As Mosca beautifully explains, we need to stop, turn within, inquire with these ten principles. Through them we'll receive our true guidance, showing us the path to harmony within ourselves and in the world. The light and intelligence within us are ever-present, always ready to illuminate our way through any darkness.

To quote Rilke, "Let everything into you: beauty and terror. Keep going. No feeling lasts forever. Nearby is the land they call Life. You will recognize it by its intensity."[5]

— Richard C. Miller, Ph.D.

Richard C. Miller, PhD, is a clinical psychologist, author, researcher, and spiritual teacher. Founder of the iRest Institute, co-founder of the International Association of Yoga Therapists, and the Institute for Spirituality and Psychology, he is the author of ***Yoga Nidra, The iRest Meditative Practice for Deep Relaxation and Healing,*** and ***The iRest Program for Healing PTSD.*** Richard has served as a consultant studying the efficacy of his meditation protocol, Integrative Restoration – iRest, on health, healing, and well-being with diverse populations including the military, incarcerated, and survivors of human trafficking; with issues including PTSD, traumatic brain injury, pain, chemical dependency and sleep disorders. Richard leads international trainings and retreats around the theme of enlightened living.

—www.iRest.org

[5] Barrows, Anita. *Rilke's Book of Hours: Love Poems to God.* 2005. Riverhead Books. NY, NY.

SEDONA SOUL STRETCH:

10 Ancient Yoga Principles to Heighten Consciousness and Performance

Why Read This Book?

Would you like to let go of limiting beliefs, learn how to be the best person you can be, and live a more fulfilling life? If I told you that you could make your life happier than you ever dreamed by learning to live ten ancient Yoga principles for harmony and peace, would you want to learn more?

Yes, I imagine you would want to know more about these tips for mastering well-being. What if I tell you that you already know them and probably have known them since kindergarten, but you may not be practicing them fully? If you want to live a balanced life between the pull of external responsibilities, your own personal needs, and the internal mind's constant critiquing, it's important to be mindful to keep yourself clear and centered.

This book discusses specific ways to apply an understanding of ten ancient Yoga principles to guide your everyday life decisions and achieve greater success. In the following chapters, you will learn how to use these proven principles to enrich your home and work life.

The recommendation is to practice all ten principles simultaneously and make them the desktop wallpaper of your mental existence. I have found that whenever I have an upset in life, it's usually due to violating one of these ten core Yoga principles. This might be the case for you, too. So, following them can help each of us become more of what we want to be.

From Your Most Positive Characteristics to Your Purest Soulful Essence

While the principles are not quite linear, they seem to build upon one another—beginning with ways to function ethically in the world and moving on to ways to access your inner essence and Divine Presence. The principles begin with Compassion for self and others and shift the focus inward to help you get in touch with your soul's connection to all beings throughout the Universe. While the goal is to practice all ten principles simultaneously, you might consider focusing on the social harmony principles first and the deeper soulful practices thereafter. It seems that in presenting the Yamas or social harmony principles first, the ancients are suggesting that we need to have peace in our interactions with others before we can delve into the deeper soulful aspects of our inner being.

The first set of five codes is based on human characteristics observed as the highest good present in everyone. These Social Harmony Characteristics guide you to practice Compassion for self and others, Truthfulness, Non-Stealing, Moderation in all things, and Non-Attachment to worldly desires and possessions. The second set of principles guides you to move more deeply within to expand your Higher Consciousness. One of my colleagues, renowned Yogi Donna Farhi, provides a wonderful name, calling them "Codes for Soulful Living."[6]

[6] https://healthy.net/2005/07/13/the-ten-living-principles-yamas-and-niyamas/

Following her lead, I refer to the second five principles as "Internal Soulful Practices." These principles guide you to practice Purity, Contentment, Discipline, Self-Study, and Surrender to a Higher Power as you realize your Oneness with the Invisible Intelligence of the Universe that affects every aspect of life.

The Origin of These Ten Yoga Principles

"Breaking Free From Mind--Patanjali states that human suffering arises because we confuse the mind with the spirit and the ego with the True Self. Freedom can be attained when we resolve this mix-up, first by understanding the nature of the mind, then by achieving the immediate experience of our True Self."

—Alberto Villoldo, Psychologist, Shaman, and Author

These ancient principles, that help us engage with our spirit and True Self, were culled from the oral tradition of wandering sages for hundreds of years Before Christ.

The sages, Yogis known as Sadhus or holy persons, taught these principles as a way to prevent human suffering. Approximately 200 years before Christ, these precepts were recorded as part of 196 wise sayings or aphorisms in ***The Yoga Sutras of Patanjali***, which has been translated with commentary by numerous authors.

While Patanjali is rumored to have been either a physician or a grammarian, little is actually known about the alleged author Patanjali, whose text is now considered the philosophical foundation of Yoga. In Part I of ***The Yoga Sutras***, Patanjali discusses many common afflictions and negative thought patterns that challenge humanity. He addresses these pitfalls to heighten our awareness and prepare us to avoid them. In Part

II, Sutra # 2, Patanjali recommends the Yoga path and contemplation as ways to focus on obstacles and minimize them. In Alistair Shearer's edition of ***The Yoga Sutras of Patanjali***, he notes that according to Sutra #2, the eight limbs of Yoga "nourish the state of samadhi [meditative union with the Divine] and weaken the causes of suffering."[7]

Before introducing the eight limbs of Yoga in Book II, Patanjali tells us in Sutra #16 that the "pain that has not yet come is avoidable."[8] Hence, we are guided to view these principles for well-being as ways to avert painful experiences.

In Part II, Sutras #29-45, Patanjali recommends ten codes of conduct to live a contented life free from suffering.[9] Calling them "the mighty universal vows, not limited by place, time, circumstance or class," Patanjali emphasizes that these values are universal and timeless.[10] Since 200 BC, these precepts have been observed and reported to help people avoid potential human afflictions and increase well-being. The principles have been widely adopted as universal codes of living in many cultures, helping those who embrace them to achieve social harmony and personal peace. Yet, these principles are not anything you need to strive toward, like the Ten Commandments. Instead, you already possess these characteristics in your inherent goodness and your highest essence. It's not about striving but about being mindful to practice these beneficial principles.

We Are What We Are Seeking

Applying these principles to daily life is not about adding anything to the way you now are. Practicing these principles is about being who you already are and harnessing the Divine connectedness you share with others

[7] Shearer, Alistair, *The Yoga Sutras of Patanjali* (New York: Bell Tower, 1982), p. 102.

[8] Satchidananda, Sri Swami, *The Yoga Sutras of Patanjali* (Virginia: Integral Yoga Publications, 1978), p.102.

[9] Iyengar, B.K.S., *Light on the Yoga Sutras of Patanjali* (California: Harper Collins, 1996), pp. 134-139.

[10] Iyengar, B.K.S., Light on the Yoga Sutras of Patanjali (California: Harper Collins, 1996), pp. 136.

and the entire Universe. When you live authentically, the Oneness you may have been seeking outside of yourself shines from the very core of your own being.

By living the first nine ancient principles for harmony and wellbeing, you can manifest your inner goodness and gain access to the Divine Light within, which is the tenth and last principle of Surrender to a Higher Power. This is the internal Higher Self—the "I am that I am"—that spiritual seekers aim to actualize in meditation. It's the part of you that provides inner guidance and feels Oneness with all of existence.

The Context of Our Ten Ancient Principles

Allow me to mention the Sanskrit terms for the two groups of these five principles to put them in context. The first group is called the *Yamas*, or Social Restraints; the second group is called the *Niyamas*, or Internal Observances. The *Yamas* and *Niyamas* constitute the first two limbs of Patanjali's system of Ashtanga (Eightfold) Yoga, in which he teaches the eight aspects of Yoga for well-being.

We mentioned earlier that as we apply these codes to modern life, we are calling the five codes for succeeding with yourself and others-- the “Social Harmony Characteristics” and the five inwardly focused principles for personal mastery the “Internal Soulful Practices.” While I am committed to authentically sharing these ancient Yoga principles, I take the liberty of including my own interpretations, elaborating on their applications, and associating each principle with aspects of Yoga class practice. Hence, the metaphor "Soul Stretch."

The first and fundamental limb of Yoga is the five *Yamas* or Social Harmony Characteristics:

1. Compassion (*Ahimsa*)—Be Centered in Your Heart
2. Truthfulness (*Satya*)—Stay Aligned
3. Non-Stealing (*Asteya*)—Keep Your Eyes on Your Own Mat

4. Moderation (*Brahmacharya*)—Don't Stretch Too Far
5. Non-Attachment (*Aparigraha*)—Relax Your Grip

Following these principles can help you stay in harmony with your integrity and the people with whom you live, work, and play.

The second limb of Yoga is the five *Niyamas* or Internal Soulful Practices:

1. Purity (*Shaucha*)—Stay Clean and Focused
2. Contentment (*Santosha*)—Smile into Each Stretch
3. Discipline (*Tapas*)—Hold the Pose Through Challenges
4. Self-Study (*Svadhyaya*)—Reflect on Your Practice
5. Surrender to a Higher Power (*Ishvara Pranidhana*)— Trust Inner Guidance and Reach High

Following these principles can help you develop a deeper personal awareness, expand consciousness, and achieve greater peace and well-being.

The Eight Limbs of Yoga

Our two sets of principles, the focus of this book, are the first two limbs of Yoga and its foundation. In case you are wondering what the other limbs might be, here are the eight limbs of Patanjali's Ashtanga (Eightfold) Yoga System:

1. *Yamas*—Social Restraints or Codes
2. *Niyamas*—Internal Observances
3. *Asanas*—Yoga Postures
4. *Pranayama*—Conscious Breathing
5. *Pratyahara*—Sense Withdrawal

6. *Dharana*—Concentration
7. *Dhyana*—Meditation
8. *Samadhi*—Transcendence

Now, let's continue to explore the application of the ten principles in the first two limbs and ponder how well you are already living them and how you might stretch to live them more fully.

Just Say, "Good Notice!"

First, a word of caution. Never use these principles to find fault with or blame yourself or others. We are all doing the best we can with the resources we have in each moment.

Be careful not to "should" yourself, as in saying you should or shouldn't do something. Also, do not resort to telling yourself you "have to" or "need to" do or stop doing anything. And don't apply the principles to anyone other than yourself—not your wife, husband, children, friends, or colleagues.

Be conscious to always treat yourself and others with Compassion (our paramount principle) as you live, learn, and grow. A dear friend, Quinta Oran, taught me to say "Good Notice!" and congratulate myself whenever I see something about myself that I would like to improve. These principles represent a high standard of behavior. You are expanding your consciousness to follow them as often as you can, as well as you can. I invite you to be patient with yourself and others when lapses occur.

Applying these principles to daily life offers a way to learn and stretch into greater success with your outer performance, inner well-being, and expanding consciousness. Let's look more deeply into the nuances and benefits of each principle. As you read the following chapters, you will find them sprinkled with quotations from famous Yoga masters, poets, authors, and scientists, as well as business, religious, and political leaders who have advocated following these beneficial principles throughout the ages.

About the Title "Sedona Soul Stretch"

Sedona Soul Stretch does not require a trip to Sedona or to any other sacred place. It is a book to guide you on a life-changing journey within, wherever you may be at the moment. I have included the name "Sedona" because so many of my own soul- stretching epiphanies have occurred here in Sedona, where the red rock vortices are believed to help raise consciousness.

Throughout the book, I relate experiences of spiritual connection that have taken place with clients in my Sedona Spirit Yoga and Hiking sessions. Hence, the title ***Sedona Soul Stretch***. However, the wisdom of these 10 Ancient Yoga Principles extends beyond time and space and will be yours forever, no matter where you find yourself in life. May living these principles help you grow most deeply and compassionately.

CONTENTS

10 ANCIENT YOGA PRINCIPLES

YAMAS
Principles for Social Harmony

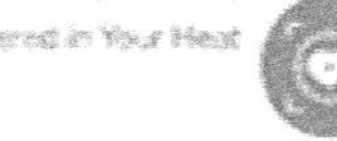

COMPASSION (AHIMSA)
Be Centered in Your Heart

TRUTHFULNESS (SATYA)
Stay Aligned

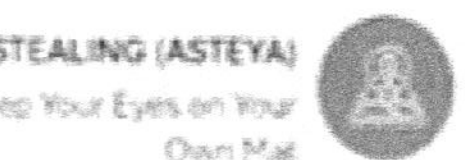

NON-STEALING (ASTEYA)
Keep Your Eyes on Your Own Mat

MODERATION (BRAHMACHARYA)
Don't Stretch Too Far

NON-ATTACHMENT (APARIGRAHA)
Relax Your Grip

NIYAMAS
Internal Soulful Practices

PURITY (SHAUCHA)
Stay Clean and Focused

CONTENTMENT (SANTOSHA)
Smile into Each Stretch

DISCIPLINE (TAPAS)
Hold the Pose Through Challenges

SELF-STUDY (SVADHYAYA)
Reflect on Your Practice

SURRENDER TO A HIGHER POWER (ISHWARA PRANIDHANA)
Trust Inner Guidance and Reach High

THE 8 LIMBS OF YOGA

Heart fully open
Witnessing all with God's grace
The lotus honors life

CHAPTER ONE

◇ ◇ ◇

Compassion—
Be Centered in Your Heart

The First Yama: The Yoga Principle
AHIMSA, Compassion and Non-Harming

How might you be kinder to yourself and others?

Our first principle is about living your life from a place of caring for yourself and others, focused within your heart. Please do not let the ills of the world damage your heart's capacity to feel, trust the Universe, and hold the highest intentions for all beings. Be open to learning to make decisions based on Compassion, reverence for all life, and a commitment to never harm anyone. Becoming centered in your heart space is a popular well-being practice that helps you attune to an "inner knowing" of what feels best to think, say, or do from a place of caring. Drop out of your head into your heart, and your life will work better! Too much thinking and too little feeling thwart success.

Did you ever hear that "Your mind is not your friend?" and "What goes around, comes back around?" Take a few moments to consider the benefits of being in your heart and feeling your connectedness to all of life instead of living in your head, conjuring thoughts that may separate you from others.

Let's explore this principle and ways you can center yourself in your heart and let your heart guide your behavior in business and society, as well as at home with yourself and your family.

Drop Out of Your Head into Your Heart

It's easy to get caught up in the incessant bombardment of the Monkey Mind's mental chatter that often keeps us too busy to see and appreciate what is right in front of us. When unable to meditate, my Sedona Spirit Yoga clients often tell me that their minds are so busy that they cannot feel any "stillness" inside. I assure them that it takes practice and invite them to do "Drop-ins." I focus on the "Drop-in" as an easy way to shift energy to the present moment. Whatever my clients and I may be doing, I invite them to pause, suggest we close our eyes, and focus on our breath as we listen to, and silently label the sounds we hear and the sensations we feel. I label the sounds and sensations in a whisper—"voices... birds... cars... the sun on your skin... the gentle breeze...."

After a few moments of silence, I ask my clients to drop into their hearts and feel whatever they may be feeling inside. Finally, I ask them to make an affirmation about something good they are claiming for themselves right now in this moment..., feel it in their hearts..., declare it three times silently to the Universe..., and then open their eyes.

Usually, when they open their eyes, they smile. That's how we drop out of our heads into being *centered in our hearts.* Afterwards, I suggest to my clients that if they keep dropping in and make the drop-ins last a bit longer and longer each time, they will be able to meditate quite effectively. At the end of each chapter, I will invite you to ponder the principle at hand, and do a Drop-In to enter the silence.

Let me briefly mention another very simple way to drop out of your head into your heart quickly. You can do so by starting to hum—yes, humming as if singing a lullaby to a baby. That's guaranteed to open the heart.

HeartMath and Heart-Brain Coherence

At the forefront of techniques to stay heart-centered is a popular worldwide science called HeartMath (Heart + Math joined as one word). This science has been researching the heart-brain connection for over twenty-five years and learning how the heart influences our perceptions, emotions, intuition, and health.[11]

Author Gregg Braden reports scientific studies on Heart-Brain Coherence, showing that the Heart Brain has sensory neurites that perform the same functions as cells in the brain, maintaining that it's important to access the knowledge in our hearts as well as our brains.[12] Science is now beginning to understand the role of neurons in the heart

[11] https://www.heartmath.com/

[12] https://www.youtube.com/watch?v=8Cd3_YGASg4

and access its wisdom. Harmonizing the heart and brain into a single potent system is reported to enhance our immune response, memory, cognition, recall, and intuition. Braden asserts that this ability to harmonize the heart and brain is key to self-regulating our biology and fostering healing.

A Simple 3-Step HeartMath Technique

Gregg Braden says the best practice is to learn to drop into your heart on a regular basis to access your heart's wisdom and higher vibration.[13]

At a Gregg Braden workshop in Sedona, I learned this simple HeartMath technique. Gregg Braden taught it as three steps to FOCUS on and told participants that we might choose to touch our hearts to bring our attention there.

The 3 SHIFTS OF HEARTMATH are:

- SHIFT FOCUS to your HEART
- SHIFT BREATHING to a very SLOW PACE
- SHIFT FEELING to GRATITUDE, APPRECIATION, CARE, or COMPASSION

First, **Focus on your Heart** center, perhaps by touching your heart. Second, **Focus on Breathing Slowly**, perhaps slowing down both the inhalation and exhalation. Third, **Focus on a Feeling such as Compassion, Caring, Gratitude, or Appreciation** while continuing to breathe slowly, remaining focused on your heart.

Try this for a few moments, and feel the shift from your head into your heart. Whatever way you may choose to do it, I invite you to drop

[13] http://www.heartmath.com

out of your head into your heart. Learn to be heart-centered, and see how much more compassionate, loving, harmonious, and joyful life can become.

Compassion Means "Feeling One With"

"Understand that Compassion is a critical factor in helping

you expand your thinking, overcome fear, and grow.

Exercise compassion daily by always acting on

the urge to help someone."

—Connie Tang, Cisco Project Management Director

The ancient code of Nonviolence or *Non-harming* teaches us to be mindful that our words and actions will not injure anyone. It guides us to look within our hearts to anticipate the consequences of our thoughts, words, and actions.

The meaning of *Non-harming* goes much further than simply not committing acts of violence. Mahatma Gandhi pointed out that this principle, called *Ahimsa* (without violence) in Sanskrit, is not merely a negative state of harmlessness, but it is a positive state of Love, of doing good even to the evil-doer.[14]

People do not often realize the broad range of what can be defined as violence or harm, such as not listening to a person speak, rudely cutting off someone, or being impatient and frustrated with a family member or co-worker. Nonviolence calls for a way of being that never hurts any creature and is unconditionally compassionate and kind.

---

[14] https://www.mkgandhi.org/articles/ahimsa-Its-theory-and-practice-in-Gandhism.html

Practicing Compassion stems from understanding the Divine nature and connectedness of all living beings. First, when you recognize that there is a single Source of all you will ever witness in our world, then you can see that everything is part of a single Creative Force. All beings are part of this Oneness, part of the same Universal Conscious Intelligence.

The nature of feeling Oneness is inherent in the word Compassion. The prefix "com" means "with," and the root "passion" means "strong feeling." Compassion means recognizing that you have feelings of connectedness with other beings. It is a deep reverence for all of life, for every living creature, that guides you to honor every being with respect and kindness, whether it is a person, an animal, an insect, or a plant.

As it is said, charity begins at home. Honoring every being with respect and kindness starts with honoring yourself first. It is important to think good, kind, loving thoughts about yourself and be aware of moments when you might lapse into self-criticism or self-sabotage. Love yourself first and radiate that caring out to others.

Compassion as Trust in the Flow of Life

"The purpose of human life is to serve, and to show Compassion and the will to help others."

—Albert Schweitzer, Nobel Prize Winner

In addition to a feeling of connectedness, the true spirit of Compassion involves trusting the process of life. Underlying Compassion is the belief that as part of the Oneness, you trust in the Divine order and timing of the flow of events. You welcome possibilities that are not part of your plan and see everything that happens in life as part of a larger orchestration of the Universe. When you are centered in your heart, your heart knows the best, most humane way to deal with the flow of events.

Trusting life's process means knowing that life brings the experiences you need to learn, grow, and develop. Sometimes they may feel like painful breakdowns, but they are always breakthroughs to greater growth and well-being. The soul needs challenges to move ahead and evolve, so that's why things shift. You attract what you need to advance yourself in the flow of events.

Life mirrors your quest to know yourself in all ways and find the balance and mastery everyone seeks. You draw people into your life to test and complement who you believe you are. Any provocations prompt you to know yourself more fully and achieve a greater level of healing.

The law of retribution or Karma ensures that the kind of energy you put out will surely come back to you, as in the common saying, "What goes around, comes back around." The harsher the projections you put on other people, the more negativity you will reap at some point in time when any boomerang you may have tossed catches up with you. Becoming compassionate and heart-centered to the core depth of being is the first principle to embrace in life.

Exploring Compassion: Unconditional Kindness

"It's your unlimited power to care and to love that can make the biggest difference in the quality of your life."

—Tony Robbins, Motivational Speaker and Author

Compassion is the mindset and heart-space of caring and behaving kindly to everyone, not just those you deem worthy, those who are well-behaved, or those you like. It means being kind even when others are nasty, rude, argumentative, or, at worst—cruel. Compassion entails seeing others in their highest good, despite outward appearances.

Compassion is often defined as "unconditional kindness." This means being good to everyone, however they might be in the moment, without requiring them to earn your respect by meeting certain criteria or standards. This means that no matter what you feel might warrant behaving in an unkind way, under all conditions, the goal is to practice Compassion. As a compassionate person, you must be open to understanding the point of view of others, to "walk a mile in their moccasins," and know that they are doing the best they can with the resources they have in the moment. You can feel empathy for someone whose behavior is unacceptable to the extent that you might think, "There but for the Grace of God, go I." Compassion means genuinely caring for others with an open heart and gentleness.

I once saw a mother yank her little daughter's arm and practically drag her tiny body down the supermarket aisle. "How horrible," I thought, wanting to reach out to rescue the child.

At the same time, I could look compassionately at the poor, frustrated mother who had erupted and lost her temper. Both needed help.

Although I do not condone her actions, I can see that perhaps if this tired, over-wrought mother could have taken some time from childcare to relax and take better care of herself, she might have had more love and patience available to give to her child.

This illustrates how important it is to be compassionate to yourself first so you can carry that kindness and care to others in your life. True Compassion is natural, sincere, and genuine when you are *centered in your heart.*

What You Do to Another, You Do to Yourself

Practicing Compassion, you treat each being with unconditional kindness as an extension of your own self and never intentionally cause harm. Based on the concept that all creatures in the Universe are one, whatever you do to another, you do to yourself. Likewise, what you do to yourself has a ripple effect on others in the interrelated energy of the Conscious Intelligence Field.

Carrying on his grandfather Gandhi's teachings, Arun Gandhi wrote about the nature of Nonviolence in his book, *Legacy of Love*. Arun Ghandi focused on five elements of Nonviolence: Love, Respect, Understanding, Acceptance, and Appreciation.[15] Following his lead, you can summon such feelings of Respect, Understanding, and Acceptance for those you might find challenging.

You can make a conscious effort to find common ground with people who seem strange to you. For example, someone you clash with at work may have children at home who are the same age as yours.

Even your worst enemy might be rooting for the same football team or enamored of your favorite musician. By staying heart-centered, you can search for a way to genuinely appreciate something about everyone.

I had a true lesson in learning to be compassionate when a stranger came to Yoga class one day, dressed like a biker in a leather outfit, with a fire-engine red sweater, heavy make-up, and fang-like fingernails polished green. Honestly, while I did not mean to judge, I was jarred by her contrast to the other classmates in casual sweatpants attire.

The lesson came when my car did not start, and this girl generously volunteered to drive me home. She turned out to be a gentle, spiritual, good-hearted soul who was a pleasure to be with! I learned from my mistake but did not blame myself.

---

[15] Gandhi, Arun, *Legacy of Love: My Education on the Path of Nonviolence* (California: Berkeley Hills Books, 2003).

As my dear friend Quinta Oran taught me, I congratulated myself for recognizing my lapse in Compassion, felt Love for my new student, and said to myself, "Good Notice!" without judgment or self-recrimination.

Practicing Compassion Starts at Home

"If you wish to be gentle with others,

first be gentle with yourself."

—Buddha

Most importantly, remember that practicing Compassion starts at home with kindness to yourself and your family. First, you must treat yourself with unconditional loving kindness. Then, extend that caring to your family, and ultimately to everyone else.

You may sometimes easily break your promises to yourself while keeping your commitments to others. The bubble bath you were looking forward to at the end of the day gets sacrificed to everything you need to do for the job, the house, and the children. Or the workout you wanted to do at the health club gets postponed again. How many times during the day do you berate yourself for something you did wrong or did not do right? And how often do you allow your bad mood to squash the spirit of family members or office associates by taking things out on them?

Learning to be more accepting and compassionate towards yourself, your loved ones, and your colleagues is the first step in embracing your innate compassionate nature. When you are *centered in your heart*, you are in touch with your own feelings and concerned about the feelings of others.

Worldwide Heart-Centered Movement and Servant Leadership in Business

"Business is like tennis. Those who serve well win."

—Ken Blanchard, American Business Consultant

For over fifty years, there has been a universal practice of businesses becoming more humanitarian and managers becoming more heart-centered. "Leading with Love," the theme of a movement called "Servant Leadership," originated in a 1970 essay entitled *The Servant as Leader* by Robert K. Greenleaf.

This ground-breaking essay was motivated by Herman Hesse's *Journey to the East*, in which a band of men on a journey are served by one among them, who happens to be the head of the Order incognito. Humanitarian Robert K. Greenleaf implemented Servant Leadership in his work at AT&T for over forty years and retired as Director of Management Research in 1964.[16] He left a strong Servant Leadership legacy when he passed in 1990. Greenleaf coined the term, spearheaded the leadership style, and created the Greenleaf Center for Servant-Leadership, now still operating in South Orange, New Jersey.

"Servant-leader ship is all about making the goals clear
and then rolling your sleeves up and doing whatever
it takes to help people win. In that situation,
they don't work for you, you work for them."

—Ken Blanchard, American Business Consultant

[16]http://www.ediguys.net/Robert_K_Greenleaf_The_Servant_as_Leader.pdf

Today Servant Leadership has become a popular business style among the largest companies, such as Starbucks, Nordstrom, and Marriott International, which are strong advocates for compassionate management, caring employee treatment, and nurturing work practices. Their goal is to empower their employee culture and families with Compassion, help prevent or ease suffering, welcome everyone's unique contribution, and prioritize employees' ongoing personal well-being.

An online blog posted in March, 2021, from Ottawa University, entitled *Five Proven Characteristics of A Servant Leader*, states that—Listening, Appreciation, Humility, Trust, and Caring are five essential servant leader attributes.[17] Whether you are an employee called upon to assist customers, a manager supervising a team of workers, or a parent raising a family, you can benefit from this humanistic approach to make everyone's ongoing personal well-being a priority, welcome individual contributions, and treat each person with Compassion, the way you feel is best in your heart.

How Full is Your Bucket?

"If you are not in the process of becoming the person you want to be, you are automatically engaged in becoming the person you don't want to be."

–Dale Carnegie, American Self-Improvement Author

Many years ago, in his *Seven Habits of Highly Effective People*, the late Stephen Covey alluded to everyone having an "emotional bank account" which could be depleted by negative drains and boosted by positive

[17] https://www.ottawa.edu/online-and-evening/blog/march-2021/5-proven-characteristics-of-a-servant-leader

experiences.[18] In their book *How Full is Your Bucket?* Tom Rath and his grandfather Donald O. Clifton use a bucket metaphor to draw attention to how well you are feeling personally (filling or draining your own emotional bucket) and how well you are making others feel (filling or draining their emotional buckets).[19]

Rath and Clifton note that every interaction makes a difference, and you need to fill your own and each other's buckets with what is right instead of what is wrong, with appreciation instead of criticism, and with kindness instead of harshness.

This great metaphor for the practice of Compassion inspires you to attend to filling your own and other people's buckets or Covey-bank accounts with satisfying emotions.

So, how are you feeling today? How full is your good-feeling-bucket? Are there any ways you mentally berate yourself or re-run times when others were unkind? How can you work at filling your own bucket and the buckets of teammates and family with more love and appreciation?

[18] Covey, Stephen R., *The 7 Habits of Highly Effective People: Powerful Lessons in Personal Change* (New York: Simon and Shuster, 1989).

[19] Rath, Tom and Clifton, Donald, *How Full is Your Bucket? Positive Strategies for Work and Life* (New York: Gallup press, 2004).

Benefits of Practicing Compassion

"If our hearts are filled with unconditional love and true forgiveness, we are sure to experience miracles in our lives."

—Michael Mirdad, Spiritual Teacher and Author

Yoga sages say that the reward for mastering Compassion is that it will make you so gentle and loving that no violence will be able to exist in your presence. As Yoga master Swami Satchidananda notes--"When the vow of *Ahimsa* is established in someone, all enmity ceases in his or her presence because that person emits harmonious vibrations."[20] Following this principle, when you have mastered unconditional kindness, any hostility or intended harm will simply fall away in your presence.

An illustration of this is found in a popular old story about the Peace Pilgrim, who walked over 25,000 miles for more than twenty-five years on a personal pilgrimage for peace. The Peace Pilgrim was the epitome of a compassionate soul whose loving heart touched and inspired all who met her. She reported riding in a car with a man who later admitted that he had originally intended to rob and possibly hurt her. Once in the Peace Pilgrim's presence, he was so moved by her Love and Compassion that he could not harm her.

This is the power that sages claim will develop in each of you when you become totally compassionate and heart-centered. Living from your heart, focused on caring, being kind and loving can only increase your peace within, your success at work, and your relationship with everyone you meet.

[20] Satchidananda, Sri Swami, *The Yoga Sutras of Patanjali* (Virginia: Integral Yoga Publications, 1978), p.130.

Everyday Lapses in Compassion

While most of us probably consider ourselves generally kind, there may be moments when we forget to be compassionate and reverent to ourselves and other creatures. See if any of these examples of lapses in Compassion may apply to you. No judgment or self-recrimination, just notice—

- "Kicking yourself" because you said something you shouldn't have said
- Looking in the mirror and judging some part of your appearance harshly
- Making a mistake and beating yourself up for it
- Becoming impatient on the phone or in stores with slow-moving assistants
- Killing harmless insects when there is no need to do so
- Getting irritable with family members or colleagues
- Never really listening to a certain person that you do not hold in high esteem
- Carrying resentment for someone's behavior you found objectionable
- Judging someone harshly for the things they confided in you
- Having prejudices against certain kinds of people

About Discussion and Journal Writing

I invite you to do journal writing or have discussions with friends to help you integrate these principles into your everyday way of being.

If you are new to journaling, allow me to give you a few tips.

1. Freely jot down your honest thoughts and feelings without any attention to grammar or spelling
2. Keep your journal with you for in-the-moment writing
3. Keep the content focused on your perceptions and intentions
4. Start with what you are thankful for and move to what you want to change
5. Do your best to refrain from whining or complaining
6. Be creative with doodling or drawing if you like
7. Reread your journal entries to see what you discover
8. Make your journal a record of your personal growth

Suggested Journal Topics

1. What are you noticing or discovering?
2. What are you grateful for?
3. What would you like to shift?
4. What are your intentions?
5. What actions are you planning to take?
6. How can you take better care of yourself?

Discussion and Journaling for Compassion-- Good Notices, Ahas, Gratitude, Fun Scribbling, Shifts, Intentions, and Self-Care

- What are your first impressions of the principle of Compassion?
- In what ways are you truly loving and accepting of yourself and others?
- Can you recall instances in which you tend to be critical of yourself? Why?
- At what times have you blamed yourself or allowed others to be unkind to you?
- For what do you need to forgive yourself or anyone else?
- How can you be more compassionate to yourself and the people in your life?

Ways to Practice Compassion

"We must be the change we wish to see."

—Mahatma Gandhi, Leader of Non-Violence

I will put the principle of Compassion into practice in my everyday life by committing to take the following steps:

- From now on, I will do my best to be heart-centered and adopt a non-harming mindset. Before speaking or acting, I will think about the consequences that my words and actions might have on others.

- I promise to accept, appreciate, and respect any challenging people, tasks, or events in my life. I will review any ways that I may have been critical of circumstances or relationships and shift to more positive ways of viewing them with Compassion and bucket-filling kindness.
- I promise to love, accept, and forgive myself unconditionally. I will release any negative thoughts or critical judgments as soon as they arise and replace them with gratitude, keeping my own bucket full.

If exploring this principle has made you decide to be a little kinder to yourself and others, you are successfully practicing Compassion.

Affirmations

- I am gentle to all beings
- I easily forgive myself and others
- I release fear and anger
- I move away from judging to loving
- I embrace all, trusting the Divine flow
- I stay centered in my heart

About "Drop Ins"

As mentioned earlier, to introduce my clients to meditation, I start by having them simply "Drop In" to a quiet place within. I know that most of my students and readers find it very difficult, if not impossible, to quiet the rampant Monkey Minds we all have, and I empathize. I, myself, was a Type A, New York coffee drinker and cigarette smoker, who first balked at the idea of having a quiet place within. You can become successful at finding this peaceful part of yourself as you practice "Drop Ins" for very brief and then longer periods of time. A friend taught me to pretend that my mind is a cottage, and to leave the windows open so that if thoughts come in, I can send them out the window.

The best way to find peace is to STOP whatever you are feeling or thinking in the moment. Take time to close your eyes, follow your breath within, and drop into your heart. As you observe your inbreath and outbreath, take a moment to observe your heart beating and feel your feelings. Draw your attention to whatever is happening outside of you, and label the sounds you hear and the sensations you feel in your body. You might feel the sun on your skin or a chill in the air. You might hear the noise of cars or people moving about. Just notice what's happening, label it, and let it be.

Ask your heart what it is feeling. Nestle into that awareness and let it be. Think of something or someone that makes your heart smile and rest into that warm feeling. It could be someone close to you, a baby, a butterfly, or a beautiful horizon.

Nestle into feeling good about yourself, embrace your aliveness, and feel joyful. Envision yourself fully living the Yoga principle you just read about, and take a moment to feel proud of yourself. Visualize yourself mastering this principle of life and achieving ultimate serenity and well-being. Feel grateful that you already have integrated this principle in every feature of your life. Know that all is well in your world and that the Universe is providing abundant goodness for you.

The Steps for a "Drop In"

1. Stop whatever you are doing
2. Find a quiet place free of disturbances
3. Follow your breath within
4. Focus on your heart's feelings
5. Label what you feel, hear, taste or smell
6. Think of people and things you love
7. Drop into a quiet place and let go of outer sensations
8. Nestle into feeling connected to a Higher Power/Divine Energy
9. Know that all is well in your world independent of circumstances
10. Acknowledge yourself for your successes in life
11. Feel the Universe providing abundant goodness for you

"Drop In" for Compassion

- Sit in a quiet place and close your eyes
- Breathe into feeling the love in your heart
- Label exterior sensations and let them go
- Nestle into a peaceful, loving place within
- Appreciate yourself for being kind and compassionate
- Thank the Universe for the goodness of life

Sprouting integrity
Growing truth from deep within
The tree stands rooted

CHAPTER TWO

Truthfulness—
Stay Aligned

The Second Yama: The Yoga Principle
SATYA, Truthfulness

How can you be more true to yourself and others?

"You must be Truthful to yourself in your actions, thoughts and speech before you set out in search of Ultimate Reality, Truth, or Love."

–Baba Hari Dass, Indian Yoga Master

As you may know, aligning the body in positions properly is an important part of Yoga practice. If your body is not aligned properly, you can injure yourself with over-strenuous stretching. Well, it's also that way with life. To succeed and prosper, you need to be aligned with what is true for you, or you can cause damage and hurt yourself. The challenge today is that so many conflicting beliefs are bombarding us via the media that it is difficult to hone in on what is true and what is not.

Yet, it is our responsibility to discover the Truth amid contrasting opinions or at least discover what is true for each of us. What Truths do you live by?

What does it mean to practice Truthfulness? It's commonly thought of as not lying, but practicing Truthfulness is much more than that.

On a personal level, it means being authentic and true to yourself. In relationships, it means being honest and forthright. And, on a larger scale, Truthfulness is the elusive Divine Order of the Universe.

Yoga is about the healthy alignment of mind, body, and spirit. Being true to yourself and speaking and acting consistently with your heart's assessment of Truth is what is meant by *staying aligned.*

The Yoga Sutras of Patanjali note that the mind engages in five distinct activities: correct perception, incorrect perception, and imagination, as well as sleep and memory.[21] The aphorisms of the ***Yoga Sutras*** urge you to be aware that what you experience is filtered through your perceptions, which may be valid or inaccurate and possibly even projections and illusions. Let's explore nuances of Truth and perception.

[21] Satchidananda, Sri Swami, *The Yoga Sutras of Patanjali* (Virginia: Integral Yoga Publications, 1978), p. 12.

Truth as Correct Perception

It is difficult to get a handle on Truth because perceptions are so subjective in nature. What you perceive is filtered through your eyes. Your eyes see what you expect to see and what you are familiar with from the past. That is to say, your filter of past experiences colors what you perceive as Truth.

An anecdote demonstrating misapprehension is the familiar tale of six blind men feeling different parts of an elephant and likening it to what they associate with that one part, never experiencing the whole. The blind man feeling the elephant's trunk said it was like a tree branch; the one touching the ear likened it to a fan, and the man stroking the elephant's tusk thought he was feeling a pipe. Similarly, several eyewitnesses to an incident often do not report it happening exactly the same way.

It's beneficial to remind yourself that your perceptions may or may not be accurate. Since everything you encounter is filtered through your experiential belief system, what you perceive to be true may or may not be correct. This is echoed by Don Miguel Ruiz Sr. and his son Don Jose Ruiz in their book, *The Fifth Agreement*, in a chapter called "The Power of Doubt," where they caution readers to "Be Skeptical, but learn to listen." Be skeptical as you listen to your own mind as well as the thoughts others communicate.[22]

In his earlier book of Toltec Wisdom, Don Miguel Ruiz Sr.'s *The Four Agreements* underscores the practice of Truthfulness by advising you to be impeccable with your word, not take anything personally, not make assumptions, and always do your best.[23]Incorrect perception may involve twisting or distorting the facts. It could entail judging based on misunderstanding the situation, projecting misconceptions upon other

---

[22] Ruiz, Don Miguel and Ruiz, Don Jose, *The Fifth Agreement: A Practical Guide to Self-Mastery* (California: Amber-Allen Publishing, 2010), p. 97

[23] Ruiz, Don Miguel, *The Four Agreements: A Practical Guide to Personal Freedom* (California: Amber-Allen Publishing, 1997).

people, or not being able to see beyond the same familiar patterns you have experienced in the past.

Was the man's friend rude in not listening to the end of his story, or did he really have an urgent reason to leave? Was the woman's employer favoring her male colleague, or was she projecting her own insecurity on her boss' behavior? Perceiving incorrectly might have any of us unjustly overreact and snowball events into negative consequences. It could lead to being defensive, deceitful, or deceptive.

The Wheel of Cause and Effect

It is important to understand that there is a Law of Cause and Effect in motion and a need to question your own perceptions of what is true. Every action prompts a reaction, and every thought sets a result in motion. You experience life as a wheel of desires creating effects.

Your thoughts create desires … that prompt actions … that cause experiences … that create impressions … that filter and effect a new cycle of thoughts … desires … experiences … and impressions. In every moment of life, you bring your old past impressions forth to color each new experience.

Let's look at the filters of a woman who wants to be in a relationship. Thoughts about finding a partner prompt a desire to meet someone who fits her pictures.

The woman's pictures are based on what she thinks are the qualities of a perfect mate. She has been creating these pictures since the early days when she grew up with her parents. All of the men in her life since childhood have left good or bad impressions. Perhaps she wants someone like her father or someone who is nothing like him.

As she meets new men, she automatically judges them based on these impressions of the past men in her life. She projects her mind's picture onto all of the new gentlemen she meets, just like a movie is projected onto a screen. Blinded by her own projections, this woman may not even recognize the true qualities that the men she meets have to offer.

Questioning Your Perceptions

"To be persuasive we must be believable;

to be believable we must be credible;

[to be] credible we must be truthful."

–Edward R. Murrow, American Journalist

In everyday life, there are times when people may misread each other's actions and add meaning to their words, projecting motives. In reality, there could be none, but they react defensively based on their misreading. It's quite easy to project your thoughts onto others and perceive what you are programmed to see through your mind's eye.

Much of what you view may be filtered through incorrect seeing or memory of past traumas and fantasies. Based on this filtering, you might tend to project onto others, coloring their actions with negative motives. Like many people, you may even magnify your perceptions into a full-blown drama.

The ***Yoga Sutras*** advise developing vigilant awareness over your thoughts and constant detachment from taking things personally. They recommend two activities--PRACTICE and NON-ATTACHMENT-- as the means to still the automatic thoughts that are often detrimental.[24] The

[24] Satchidananda, Sri Swami, *The Yoga Sutras of Patanjali* (Virginia: Integral Yoga Publications, 1978), p. 18.

more you become aware of watching what you think, say, and do, the more you become the witness who can observe the need to shift, detach from what you are experiencing, and adjust your behavior accordingly. You can learn to still the automatic thought patterns if you practice stepping back and examining your assumptions.

To illustrate over-dramatizing, imagine that an older brother, Peter, learns from his father that his mother has been shopping with Rick, the younger brother with whom he has had a history of rivalry. Peter views this simple report through the filter of jealousy and competitiveness he has always had toward his younger sibling.

Very quickly, it escalates in his mind into thoughts of his mother showering his brother with favoritism and Rick's taking advantage of their mother's goodhearted generosity by manipulating her into buying expensive gifts. Peter dramatizes the event to prove that his mother does love Rick more than she loves him and that Rick is greedy and manipulative.

So, what is the Truth? The mother was buying something for her younger son, and his older brother became envious and projected his own jealousy and fears, coloring both his brother's and his mother's actions with selfish motives and agendas. Of course, when people like Peter engage in such drama, they are usually unaware that they are doing it. They get caught up in their heads and forget to be heart-centered. In such times, the best anyone can do is to start to question your perceptions. Ask yourself if what you are thinking and believing is true. And, hopefully, you can learn always to give the other person the benefit of the doubt.

The Vastness of Universal Truth

"The Truth is rarely pure and never simple."

—Oscar Wilde, Irish Poet and Playwright

There are many dimensions to Truthfulness. This chapter explores the meaning of Truth on three levels--

- In the vastness of the Universe
- In our interactions with self and others
- Inside our core being

On a universal scale, Truth is so vast a concept that it is difficult to capture in words. Truth is the Divine Oneness that holds everything together. Truth is infinite and seems colored only by the human ability to access it at any given time. Each of us has our own crayons and coloring book to fill in the scenes of our lives as we learn lessons. We perceive things from the subjective point of view that we have built over the years. It is our fortress of constructed beliefs.

There are myriad points of view, perceptions, and projections through which everyone filters the Truth, so it is hard to pin down the absolute Truth without anything added. Your subjective perceptions may change as your growth lessons come. As you learn, you incorporate the new information and subsequently alter your worldview. You can sometimes have such strong beliefs about something that you are absolutely reluctant to see the other side. However, you may still gain new knowledge and completely shift your beliefs.

Take, for instance, the case of a management team member who questioned the value of a new policy about to be adopted by his department and felt honor-bound to speak against its future implementation. Then after it was instituted, he was impressed that it worked well and saw it as an efficient improvement. Incorporating the new rewarding experience, he shifted to being a staunch supporter of the same policy he had once been vehemently against. Such shifts in perception are common as you remain open to new information and integrate it into your mindset. One day's knowing may give way to another day's knowing — apparently a different Truth altogether. Thus, as you grow, your perception of Truth changes.

Truth in Your Relationships

While the infinite universal Truth seems elusive, the easiest Truth to grasp is being truthful in your interactions with yourself and others. This means doing your best to be honest as long as you do not violate the paramount principle of reverence and Compassion for all.

It means you do not speak untruths or exaggerations which distort the Truth. You do not withhold information that is in the highest good to be known. You do not start gossiping or allow others to gossip in your presence. Practicing Truthfulness means keeping your word to yourself and others and fulfilling your commitments as honestly as possible.

As you practice Truth, you do your best to make your behavior genuine and honest, devoid of deceit and projections. Being committed to Truthfulness also means that you remain open to understanding another's perceptions of what is true, allowing for differences in point of view.

Sometimes this may take the form of listening with an open mind to an opposing argument. It means that you take time to listen to, respect, and truly hear the person with whom you vehemently disagree at that moment. It entails a commitment to discover common ground when points of view clash. When communicating, it is important to both speak and listen to what is true for each other in a respectful way. However, if speaking the Truth will potentially hurt another, our primary principle of Non-harming would recommend remaining silent. Practicing Compassion and Truthfulness requires that you be kind to yourself and others and patient with your progress. You do your best to stay aligned and clearheaded, aware of your feelings, thoughts, speech, and actions so that your behavior consistently reflects Truth, clarity, and kindness.

As you move from lesson to lesson throughout life, it is vitally important, to tell the Truth to yourself and admit any mistakes or conflicts on your part. If any past experiences continue to upset you despite efforts to release them, then there are usually two causes to explore. If a past event still haunts you, either there is something you have not told the full truth about or something for which you have not forgiven yourself or another person.

So, if an issue continues to plague you, see if there is any detail you might not have told the full Truth about or anything you need to forgive yourself or another person for. Telling the full Truth and engaging in total forgiveness for everyone involved, especially yourself, will generally clear up any issue. I have found that once I tell the truth about something that did not work well and honestly accept responsibility for my role in it, the whole thing lightens up and is no longer an issue for me.

The Truth Shall Set You Free!

"The Truth will set you free,

but first it will make you miserable."

–James A. Garfield, 20th United States President

On the last evening of one of my retreats, a participant shared her disappointment that the retreat had not helped her decide whether or not to break up with her boyfriend. I invited her outside to sit on a swing with me and share her concerns about her relationship. Then I asked her to answer my questions quickly and truthfully. She agreed and blurted out fast responses as I repeated the same question a number of times — "Why are you with him?"

After hearing several responses indicating that the relationship was unfulfilling for her, I asked her to look within and see if having him in her life was a "Yes" or a "No." She immediately answered an emphatic "No!" However, as she continued to talk, I could hear that she was not ready to leave him. Her words suggested that she would probably stay with him and wind up punishing herself for doing so afterward. I obtained her permission to reflect back to her what I was hearing —

"So, you are in a relationship with someone who comes over for intimacy and leaves when you want him to stay. You try to break up with him. Then when you go out seeking another relationship and do not find one, you run back to him because he is better than nothing. Now you say you probably will go running back to him when he calls, and you will feel bad about it later."

"Okay, let's tell the Truth about this. You know that this is not a fulfilling relationship, but you are not ready to give up the little attention you are receiving. And you don't have to! Is that about right?"

Suddenly, she lightened up and began smiling. In telling the truth, she gave herself permission to have those conflicting feelings. As the old adage says, "The truth shall set you free."

I did not advocate staying with him or leaving. I simply suggested that she tell herself the Truth about how it is now and work on building strength and trust in herself. As in this situation, there may be times when your opinions and actions contradict each other. You may be incongruent, out of alignment, saying one thing and doing another.

If you continue to do something that you think is ultimately not good for you but are not ready to stop it, it would be beneficial to admit the dilemma, at least to yourself, and perhaps get some professional support to help you become clearer and stronger. If my retreat client is going to be with her boyfriend, it would be best for her to enjoy it without berating herself. Simply recognizing that a shift is needed marks the beginning of having it happen.

Tapping Inner Truth

Along with your commitment to Truth in your behavior with others, you have the opportunity to access the Truth within. At any moment in time, you can become still, stop your mental chatter, focus on your breath, and explore your inner knowing for answers to your questions. By consciously observing the breath coming through the tips of your nostrils, filling the body, inflating and deflating your diaphragm as you slowly exhale, you can use the breath to still your thoughts and get in touch with your core consciousness.

Concentrating on your breath can help you access the Truth and inner knowing that can only be found in the silence within when you tap into your core consciousness. This is the witnessing awareness that tells you what is a "Yes" is and what is a "No" and gives you guidance on the direction that would be best to take. Sometimes you need to be patient to discover the steps to guide you in that direction. Speaking and acting consistently with the knowledge of your core consciousness is staying aligned with the Truth as you see it.

Through stillness, you access the inner wisdom that is your individual connection with the universal Truth. Everyone is made of this inner Truth. With conscious practice, you can learn to become quiet and check in with your inner wisdom for guidance. When you are in touch with this inner knowing, you live in harmony, integrity, and total alignment. There are also various kinesiology techniques for muscle testing your body to find out whether or not something is in the highest good. Tapping into an inner sense of Truth is the way to affirm that what you know to be true is indeed so.

Have you ever ignored your gut feeling of something that was right for you to do and had to deal with the repercussions of going against your inner knowing? Have you ever felt that taking action was a "No," but went ahead and said "Yes" to be agreeable and then suffered unpleasant consequences?

When your heart says "No," and you go ahead and say "Yes," you are out of alignment with your true self. You can learn to practice looking somewhere inside yourself (other than in your head) for the answers to your questions.

In my professional practice as a retreat facilitator, my retreat clients often face issues they cannot resolve. I always suggest that they become quiet, breathe into their inner stillness, and let go of all thoughts. I invite them to pose their dilemma in the form of a yes-or-no question and ask themselves, "Is this a yes or a no for me?" Almost always, the response to this technique of inner questioning is a clear "yes" or "no." Then the details about how to work out the situation can be slowly discovered by checking into this core knowledge of your inner being. It's the "Yes" or "No" that's liberating. Once declared, this lessens confusion and increases awareness, allowing steps to unfold when your mind is peaceful during waking hours or sleep.

Sometimes, a client receives a clear response but is not ready to act upon it. For example, he might need to quit a job that is draining or demoralizing but may not have the resources to take action on that inner knowing. In such instances, it is best to exercise Compassion and tell yourself the Truth that you are not yet ready to do what needs to be done. By accepting that you are not yet ready to act, you can seek support and prepare to take appropriate action in the future.

Being Authentic

"Honesty is more than not lying. It is Truth telling, Truth speaking, Truth living, and Truth loving."

–James E. Faust, LDS Church Leader and Politician

Practicing Truthfulness is so much more than not lying. It is a commitment to being genuine, clear, and consistently aligned with what's true for you. So many times, people can hide behind being confused. It's your job to unravel any confusion you might experience. You may not always know exactly what steps to take or have the courage to take any steps, but you can tell the Truth about it. Once an issue becomes clear, life finds a way of moving toward its resolution.

Making something visible is the first step toward healing it. Above all, everyone needs to tell the Truth about having a "shadow side." You all have your great qualities and strengths, your "shining" aspects that are bright and wonderful. Then you also have your unwanted tendencies, your so-called "dark" or "shadow" side. This latter part of you draws in challenging experiences to help you heal and grow.

The "dark side" is any weaknesses, bad habits, short fuses, irritability, baser tendencies, or "bucket drainers" you may be personally battling. Your shadow side is any and all of the attributes and behaviors that can pull you down and make you feel bad about yourself.

All of us face the difficulty of being truthful about weaknesses we would rather not recognize. Yet, if we want to transcend these less desirable elements of our character, we need the courage to be truthful about acknowledging their presence.

It is best to recognize and admit the "shadow" tendencies you are working on as you learn life's lessons. And you also need to know when you can heal the issues yourself and when it would be best to seek professional help.

Living Truthfulness is a commitment to be true to yourself as well as true to others. It entails a commitment to finding common ground when points of view differ. *Staying aligned* and being true to yourself means you inquire into your own needs. You learn to investigate the motivations behind your actions. Why are you doing what you do? Do you agree simply to get approval or feel secure? What would be truly best and most rewarding for you? Being true to yourself entails both recognizing and fulfilling your personal desires. What do you really want?

You must learn NOT to say "Yes" in order to get someone's approval when you really want to say "No." Some people give in and do things they would rather not do.

For example, a health-conscious man, who wants to go out for a snack at the local Natural Foods Store, might give in and go for the usual fast-food burger drive-in again upon his companion's insistence. Or a wife might let her husband persuade her to see another war movie even though they both know that she gets tense watching extreme violence and bloodshed.

A person who cannot say "No" might get overwrought with time-consuming tasks that need to be done to please others. To live well, you have to discover what your needs are and do your best to fulfill them. Honoring your own preferences, you can learn to express and fulfill your needs and desires in harmony with others in your surroundings. Being true to yourself and genuine with others — that is living Truthfulness.

Benefits of Staying Aligned in Truthfulness

According to the ***Yoga Sutras,*** Truthfulness in thought, word, and deed is the highest virtue. Yoga master B. K. S. Iyengar notes that when one "is firmly established in the practice of truth, his/her words become so potent that whatever he/she says comes to a realization."[25] Imagine being so powerful that whatever you say is true becomes manifested.

Swami Satchidananda echoes this belief in the power of Truthfulness, claiming that, by embodying the quality of Truth, "Yogis get the power to attain for themselves and others the fruits of work without doing the work. … things come to them automatically. All nature loves an honest person. With the establishment of honesty, the state of fearlessness comes. One need not be afraid of anybody and can always lead an open life. When there are no lies, the entire life becomes an open book."[26]

Such is the great power to effortlessly manifest one's desires through the practice of Truthfulness and honesty. And, as discussed earlier, "the truth shall set us free!" Whenever you come to an honest reckoning of any situation or experience, you liberate yourself from any challenges it may have formerly presented. Being firmly established in the practice of Truth leads to a life of harmony, integrity, and powerful manifestation. Living and sharing your authentic Truth builds strong relationships, career success, and ongoing contentment.

[25] Iyengar, B.K.S., *Light on the Yoga Sūtras of Patañjali* (California: Harper Collins, 1996), p. 142.

[26] Satchidananda, Sri Swami, *The Yoga Sutras of Patanjali* (Virginia: Integral Yoga Publications, 1978), p. 131.

Everyday Lapses in Truthfulness

Most of us think of ourselves as "pretty honest" people. However, let's look at some everyday examples of times when we may be unaware that we are not fully practicing Truthfulness. See if any of the following examples may apply to you at times, but do not judge or blame yourself; just notice--

- Telling lies so that you will not hurt a person's feelings
- Saying "Yes" when you really want to say "No"
- Omitting the part of the Truth you would rather not tell
- Making excuses for not doing something you committed to do
- Getting angry and blaming it on the other person
- Having a hidden agenda for doing nice things
- Glossing over your mistakes to make yourself look better
- Letting someone talk you out of doing something that would be good for you
- Letting someone talk you into something you know would not be good for you
- Taking credit for something you did not actually do yourself

Discussion and Journaling for Truthfulness-- Good Notices, Ahas, Gratitude, Fun Scribbling, Shifts, Intentions, Self-Care

- What insights do you have about the principle of Truthfulness?
- In what ways are you most truthful and genuine to people in your life?
- How might you be more true to yourself and your inner desires?
- At what times are you less than fully honest in your interactions and relationships?
- Can you recall a time you did not "walk your talk" or follow up on what you said you would do?
- How can you be more truthful to yourself and your relationships?

Ways to Practice Truthfulness

I will put the principle of Truthfulness into practice by making a commitment to take the following steps:

- I vow to be true to myself and compassionately honest with what is so for me. I will make decisions based on my authentic inner knowing.
- I promise to step back and take a second look at the Truthfulness of any of my perceptions that seem to judge people and experiences –whether negatively or positively.
- I commit to maintaining the highest Truth in my thoughts, words, and actions and being compassionately honest with others.

Now that you are more conscious of being true to yourself and honest with people, you are already experiencing the benefits of Truthfulness.

Affirmations

- I am clear about who I am
- I am committed to being my word
- I speak my Truth appropriately
- I listen to and respect the Truth of others
- I am always true to myself
- I am grounded in integrity and harmony

"Drop In" for Truthfulness

- Sit in a quiet place and close your eyes
- Breathe into feeling the love in your heart
- Label exterior sensations and let them go
- Nestle into a peaceful, loving place within
- Appreciate yourself for being honest and truthful
- Thank the Universe for the goodness of life

Coveting nothing
Trusting Divine abundance
The well keeps filling

CHAPTER THREE

Non-Stealing—
Keep Your Eyes on Your Own Mat

The Third *Yama*: The Yoga Principle *ASTEYA*, Non-Stealing

How can you more fully practice honoring what belongs to others?

In Yoga class practice, it's human nature to look over at the other students on the mats next to yours and compare yourself to them and perhaps covet their agile bodies. Instructors guide students to focus on their own mat and pay attention to their own performance. It's much the same in daily life as we tend to look at what others may possess or accomplish and wish we were in their shoes. Or forsaking Compassion, we might be thankful that we are not as bad off as they are. Are there times that you compare yourself to others? Have you ever even momentarily coveted anyone's possessions or achievements? Can you recall ever looking enviously at someone who is masterfully performing a feat you can barely muster? Our third principle of ancient Yoga wisdom guides you to *keep your eyes on your own mat*, which is good advice to incorporate into your life.

Honor What Belongs to Others

"Honesty is the cornerstone of character. The honest man or woman seeks not merely to avoid criminal or illegal acts, but to be scrupulously fair, upright, fearless in both action and expression. Honesty pays dividends both in dollars and in peace of mind."

—B. C. Forbes, Financial Journalist,

Founder of Forbes Magazine

This principle stems from the ancient Yoga code of Non-Stealing, called *Asteya* in Sanskrit. To create harmony with others and develop integrity within ourselves, it is important to not steal, or in positive terms, to honor what belongs to others, and *keep your eyes on your own mat.*

Stealing or coveting what others have implies a scarcity consciousness, suggesting that there is not enough for everyone. This principle teaches that each person has the power to manifest whatever s/he may need, so there is no reason to take anything from another without permission. This concept is based on believing and trusting in the universal flow of abundance rather than fearing that you will not have enough of what you need.

Each of us has our wellspring to tap into. When you see others prosper, you can be genuinely happy for their success instead of expressing envy or coveting what they have. At times, you may feel that you are receiving less than your due share of riches, and perhaps this is true if your current circumstances or economic pressures reflect that. It is essential to learn to nip such negative thinking in the bud and shift to a more positive attitude so that you do not attract more lack with scarcity thinking. Remember the axioms: "You get what you think" and "You get what you believe."

If you believe that "There is nothing out there for me," you will attract more of "There's nothing out there for me." The secret is to maintain a belief in the possibility of greater future prosperity, even in the face of hardship. You can shift your focus from bewailing what you believe is missing to feeling grateful for all that you already have in your life. As you hold positive thoughts about what you are attracting and manifesting, you can be generous to others and glad to see them prosper.

One of my teachers, Terri Cole-Whittaker, author of *What You Think of Me is None of My Business,* shares how she responds when she sees someone having something she desires. Rather than feeling jealous, she likes to exclaim, "That's for me!" whenever she sees another person having something she wants.[27] It's as if she is calling the prosperous situation to manifest in her life. It feels good to claim "That's for me" and believe you are attracting good fortune rather than being envious of another having it. Try it.

[27] Cole-Whittaker, Terri, *What You Think of Me is None of My Business* (California: Berklely, 2020).

Trust the Universal Flow of Abundance

"If we are completely free from stealing and greed,

contented with what we have, and if we keep serene minds,

all wealth comes to us. If we do not run after it,

before long, it runs after us."

–Sri Swami Satchidananda, Indian Yoga Master

Having a positive attitude and stretching into this principle calls for trusting that there indeed is a universal flow of abundance and investing your energy for the highest good. You can learn to trust that you are always taken care of and that the seeds you are planting will come to fruition. Believing that everyone has a share of life's good fortune and setting intentions to manifest your desires, you can express genuine joy instead of jealousy for those around you who are prospering. I recall counseling a client who had given up her apartment due to the loss of her job. No longer earning money to pay the rent, she was moving from one family of friends to another for sleepovers. She told me how hard it was to have lost her home, and I empathized. Then I asked her if she at least realized how lucky she was to have a handful of friends who warmly welcomed her to stay over, dine with their family, and sleep in their home.

This question shifted her thoughts from complaint to gratitude and created an opening for me to discuss future options with her. She was able to compose intentions to fulfill her needs and desires. She let go of feeling unworthy and started believing that better circumstances would come. I encouraged her to be more confident as she looked for employment, which she shortly found. The turning point came when she stopped feeling bad about herself and presented herself as someone who does have a lot to offer.

There is the stretch of this principle—trusting that the well is full and there's enough water for everyone, including you. Set strong intentions, and try different ways to dip your bucket until it fills to a desirable level.

Stretching into greater life success with this principle involves respecting what belongs to others beyond the physical realm of possessions. This principle addresses the many more subtle ways you can tend to misappropriate energy, such as harming a person's reputation by spreading gossip, sabotaging a meeting with your personal agenda, or taking credit for something another accomplished—just to give a few examples. Let's look at applying this wisdom in terms of respecting each other's possessions, relationship commitments, creative contributions, roles, and time agreements.

Possessions

First, the obvious place to start a discussion of non-stealing is with concrete possessions. While most of us do not rob banks, we sometimes take home things that do not belong to us. No matter how small the item may be, if you do not have expressed permission to take it home, that constitutes stealing. Following this principle, you do not take possession of anything without the owner's or boss' consent. You do not take more than your due share of resources. Hoarding more than what is rightfully yours creates problems, causes animosity, and lowers self-esteem.

You can heighten your consciousness to respect the property of others, whether it be returning that library book or video, leaving items belonging to a hotel at the hotel, refraining from taking clerical supplies home from work, or remembering to give back something you borrowed. Are there any such items you can ever recall taking home without permission? I believe I may still have a few pencils and notepads I casually took home from a job I had decades ago. This principle also calls for exploring times you may have been jealous or coveted something belonging to another, such as a luxurious car, a lavish home beyond your current means, or even a colleague's new promotion that you wanted for yourself. Instead of focusing on what is missing, you can turn your attention to the many ways you are blessed with abundance by focusing on what you already have. You can remember to be grateful for the ease of driving the trusty car you now own, the many comforts of your small, affordable home, and the different ways you are shown respect by management in your current job role. *Gratitude is always the great soother that takes us from gripe to grace.*

Relationships

"Give the respect you want to receive; embody the grace you hope to encounter; and help others with no expectations whatsoever."

—Cory Booker, New Jersey Senator

A more subtle form of stealing occurs in everyday relationships with others when boundaries are not respected. At times, people squash another's energy by saying something negative, trying to control what's happening, or drawing attention to themselves. Unfortunately, this happens too often. For example, someone might repeatedly interrupt a speaker or jump in with the punch line of someone else's joke, as husbands and wives often do. You can be mindful not to usurp your partner's stories or your colleague's presentations, not take over the center stage at another's birthday party, and not make inappropriate advances towards an attractive person who is in a committed relationship.

Likewise, there is no flirting with a friend's new date or overstepping boundaries to attract attention. It is called honoring relationships, and it's beneficial to realize that when people gossip about another, they are "stealing" respect from that person by repeating bad things about them.

Have you ever felt uncomfortable when you ran into someone about whom you have just heard damaging gossip? Most times, you would find that the gossip was nothing but a false rumor. I invite you to make a commitment not to allow gossip in your presence. Stop the gossip by making a nice comment about the guy or gal being talked about and get the conversation to shift in a more positive direction.

At your job, you can refrain from accepting credit for the work completed by a colleague. Can you see any ways that you might stretch into showing greater respect for others and, in doing so, greater respect for yourself?

Creative Contributions

"Avoid any kind of mis-appropriation of material or non-material things, such as acceptance of undeserved praise. When non-stealing is perfected, one is freed from the illusion of ownership: me/mine, you/yours."

—Baba Hari Dass, Indian Yoga Master

Though the lines may be a bit blurry at times, this guideline of honoring what belongs to others, or *keeping your eyes on your own mat*, applies to your contributions at work and in the community. There needs to be an element of respect for the authorship of documents written, the creation of projects initiated, and the design of events led. As mentioned earlier, it's unfair to accept praise for doing a great job when the proper action is to acknowledge the colleague who did most of the work.

When I worked in public education, I recall being an assistant to the English Department Chairperson and having my work "appropriated" by a new supervisor who came in to head the Department. She put her new heading on all of the original teaching strategy documents that I had composed for the Department, deleting my byline that had been prominently displayed.

She definitely had no awareness of the propriety of respecting my original work. This is just one of my lessons, and I am sure some of you can immediately think of several of your own. But unfortunately, this kind of misappropriation is common in organizations and speaks to the need for everyone to honor each other's original creative contributions with greater acknowledgment and appreciation.

Honoring Roles

"Having clear boundaries means that we are in touch enough with the healthy, loving part of ourselves to know what does and doesn't work for our higher good, and to choose accordingly."

—Michael Mirdad, Spiritual Teacher and Author

Each of us plays many roles at home and at work. Therefore, the principle of honoring boundaries calls for respecting the parameters of people's various roles in life. For example, when a family visits a neighbor and their child misbehaves with the host's child, it's the parent's responsibility to discipline their daughter and not appropriate for the neighbor to chastise her.

At the office, it's not proper for any employee to ask the manager's private secretary to do a few clerical tasks unless the manager knows about it and consents. Also, it's the receptionist's job to answer incoming calls and not tell a colleague to answer them for her so she can finish typing. Another example, closer to home, is the babysitter who tells the child needing her attention to go and play while she is absorbed talking to her boyfriend on the phone. Not performing the roles assigned to you or infringing upon the roles of others are examples of "stealing" energy. Essentially, people's roles are to be respected as boundaries. What are your examples of roles needing greater respect in your life?

Time Promised

Perhaps the most subtle violation of honoring what belongs to others is stealing time. There is the time at work that we use for personal phone calls and emails, the extra-long lunches that include shopping and errands, and the work time lost when we duck out early to go to the dentist and still get the full day's pay.

Especially now that the pandemic has caused many businesses to put employees on the "honor system" to do some office work at home, it is vital that everyone focuses on delivering the time promised and reporting with integrity.

Honoring employment time means staying present to give the tasks of your work day your full attention. If we look, I am sure each of us can find instances in which we took care of personal needs at the expense of a job—whether at the office or at home.

I must confess that when I did occasional substitute teaching in Sedona decades ago, I would sometimes sit at the front classroom desk folding my Yoga retreat brochures. I was doing so while the students completed assigned work instead of walking around the room more frequently to check on them. Now I would give the job I had taken for the day my 100% attention—no blame, just "good notice."

Often in families, parents or siblings promise to do something with a child and do not honor that time. An example might be the divorced father or mother who brings his or her daughter along to do errands instead of giving the child quality time during the one weekend they have together.

Another illustration is the person who is always late and makes everyone wait for him or her. That's a real subtle drain on everyone's time and energy. A further example is urgent calls to friends when feeling upset and needing to ventilate, expecting them to drop everything and listen without asking if this is a good time for them to hear what's going on with you.

These are just a few examples of not honoring others in daily interactions. How well have you established your boundaries? How can you *keep your eyes on your own mat* and become more respectful of the boundaries of team members, friends, family, and others?

Benefits of Keeping Your Eyes on Your Mat

"We are all one family in the world. Building a community that empowers everyone to attain their full potential through each of us respecting each other's dignity, rights and responsibilities— makes the world a better place to live."

—Pope John Paul II

The ancients claimed that great wealth comes to a person who fully honors what belongs to others. As Yoga master B.K.S. Iyengar notes, "When abstention from stealing is firmly established, precious jewels come. Upon the man who does not take what does not belong to him, all riches are showered. Being without desire, he effortlessly attracts what is precious, materially and figuratively, including the gem of all jewels, virtue.[28]

Life works better when you have harmony or what Shamanism calls "right relationship" with family, friends, and colleagues. You create better bonds with people when you authentically fulfill your roles and set healthy boundaries while you honor and respect the roles and boundaries of others. Trusting in the bounty of the Universe and refraining from hoarding, envying, or stealing builds your confidence and self-esteem, as well as the trust of your peers. Living with the understanding that the Universe will bless you helps to manifest your desires and cultivate ongoing contentment and joy.

Everyday Lapses in Respect for Belongings

"Honesty isn't any policy at all;

it's a state of mind, or it isn't honesty."

—Eugene L'Hote, Postmaster for President Lincoln

While I am sure that most of you generally do practice respect for what belongs to others, it's beneficial to explore any areas in which you might shift to having greater regard. Let's look at some common examples of not respecting others. See if any of these examples apply to you—

- Bringing things home from the job without permission
- Accepting credit for something you did not do

[28] Iyengar, B.K.S., *Light on the Yoga Sutras of Patanjali* (California: Harper Collins, 1996), p. 144.

- Cutting off or interrupting the person speaking
- Copying someone's creative work without proper acknowledgment
- Stealing the spotlight from the host of the event
- Using time on the job for personal purposes
- Not spending time promised with a loved one
- Borrowing something and not returning it
- Taking more than your share of anything
- Sampling store candy or snacks that you did not pay for

Discussion and Journaling for Non-Stealing—Good Notices, Ahas, Gratitude, Fun Scribbling, Shifts, Intentions, and Self-Care

- What comes to mind when you reflect on Non-Stealing?
- Can you enumerate ways you feel blessed with abundance or a "full well"?
- In what areas of life do you feel that the Universe is not providing for you?
- Is there anyone you are jealous of or have envied in the past? Why?
- Is there anything you borrowed or used inappropriately that you might make amends for?
- How can you show greater respect for the belongings and accomplishments of others?

Ways to Practice Respect for Self and Others

I will apply this principle of *keeping my eyes on my own mat* and show greater respect for myself and others by making a commitment to take the following steps:

- I will be conscious to ask permission before taking time off from a job for personal purposes or taking any items home for my private use.
- I promise to honor people's self-expression with my full attention and do my best not to repeat derisive comments or gossip.
- I will make sure to people's relationships and accomplishments and not covet anyone's possessions or successes.

As you become more respectful of the possessions, roles, and boundaries of others, you are set to reap the rewards of Non-Stealing.

Affirmations

- I respect people's ideas and accomplishments
- I honor what belongs to others
- I am grateful for what I have
- I appreciate my abundance
- I am whole and complete
- I am at peace with myself and others

"Drop In" for Non-Stealing

- Sit in a quiet place and close your eyes
- Breathe into feeling the love in your heart
- Label exterior sensations and let them go
- Nestle into a peaceful, loving place within
- Appreciate yourself for respecting what belongs to others
- Thank the Universe for the goodness of life

Brahmacharya

Loving God foremost
Pleasures and desires bow
To the Light within

CHAPTER FOUR

Moderation—
Don't Stretch Too Far

The Fourth *Yama*: The Yoga Principle *BRAHMACHARYA*, Energy Moderation

In what ways might you practice greater moderation?

Do you feel exhausted when attempting to complete simple chores on your to-do list?

Do you feel frustrated that you cannot manage to get everything on your day's agenda done? Do you ever wonder what you might change to have more energy throughout the day?

"In moderating, not satisfying desires, lies peace."

—Ben Hecht, American Screenwriter

It's beneficial to reflect upon how you use your energy to either boost or drain your vitality. Also, it is healthy to ponder what consumes most of your time and what or whom you neglect when tasks overflow and create a time shortage. For example, what proportion of your time do you spend at work or on work-related projects, relaxing at home with family, or nurturing yourself with healthy hobbies and growth opportunities?

Do you know how to nurture yourself when your energy drops from too much time glued to the computer or a very long day filled with emotionally exhausting challenges? Are you aware of when you need self-nurturing and how to provide it for yourself? In what ways do you *stretch too far* and waste your energy in unrewarding ways? Let's take a look.

Practicing Moderation and Balance

"Everything in balance, everything in moderation –

try not to go over the top in any direction but

be free to explore and enjoy. Live heart-fully."

—Jay Woodman, English Poet and Artist

This fourth principle teaches you to control and channel life force energy by practicing moderation and balance. Your energy is your most precious asset. It is important to conserve your life force energy and direct it to the most beneficial uses. This principle calls for you to show greater respect for yourself by staying mindful that your vital energy flow needs to be nurtured and regenerated. You can become alert to how you squander and renew your life force and choose to replenish it when needed. As you become accustomed to checking on your level of vitality, you can alert yourself to adjust your energy intake and expenditure when it is about to be depleted by *stretching too far.*

This concept of energy management stems from the ancient Yoga principle called *Brahmacharya.* This Sanskrit term denotes the first of four stages of traditional Indian life, whereby students remained celibate up to the age of twenty-five as they focused on studying scriptures and learning skills. It was believed that refraining from sex would provide greater life force to channel to higher goals.

Have no fear; I am not advocating celibacy! In modern times, this principle stands for the ideal energy balance achieved through moderation or *not stretching too far.* It has come to mean proper conduct, conscious sexuality, moderation of sensual desires, life force conservation, and channeling energy to higher purposes.

Channeling Sex Energy

"In the art of sacred sexuality, our bodies meet to physically express what is felt in our hearts and souls."

—Michael Mirdad, Spiritual Teacher and Author

Sexual energy is a very powerful expression of the life force, and the ***Yoga Sutras*** teach that abstinence, at times, can help us channel that energy towards greater accomplishment. While almost all of the famous Yogis were married and had children, they also learned and taught followers to conserve and direct their sexual energy to achieve higher goals without diminishing the enjoyment of pleasure when engaged in sexuality.

This principle does not mean that you have to avoid sex. Instead, it urges becoming mindful about engaging in sex and not allowing excesses to dissipate your vitality. Sexual union can be a sacred channeling of energy between two beings united in their Highest Consciousness.

The recommendation is that you consider sex to be a sacred interaction and treat it as such by practicing "conscious" sexuality rather than casual or careless sex. This principle invites you to look at how you use your sensual and sexual energy and become more aware of how you dissipate your strength in general. So, let's dive deeper into understanding the vital life force energy that drives our existence.

Prana or Life Force

"It's a universe made out of energy,

everything is entangled; everything is one."

—Bruce H. Lipton, Developmental Biologist

While you live in a physical body composed of organs, blood vessels, and cells, you are also composed of an energy or life force called *Prana* in Sanskrit. According to B.K.S. Iyengar, this life force or *Prana* —

"... permeates each individual as well as the Universe at all levels. It acts as physical energy; as mental energy, where the mind gathers information; and as intellectual energy with a discriminative faculty, where information is examined and filtered. The same Prana acts as sexual, spiritual, and cosmic energy."

"All that vibrates in the Universe is Prana: heat, light, gravity, magnetism, vigor, power, vitality, electricity, all beings and nonbeings. It is the prime mover of all activity. It is the wealth of life. This self-energizing force is the principle of life and of consciousness. It is the creation of all beings in the Universe. All beings are born through it and live by it.... Prana is the fundamental energy and the source of all knowledge."[29]

How can you maintain a steady stream of this powerful energy? One way is through conscious breath control to increase the amount of *Prana* or life force you breathe in. The science of breath control called *Pranayama* (a Sanskrit word meaning an extension of the *Prana* or life force) is the fourth limb of Patanjali's eight-limbed Ashtanga Yoga to prevent human suffering.

(See the introduction for the Eight Limbs of Yoga.) *Pranayama* teaches exercises to exhale more slowly for deeper relaxation and to inhale faster for greater energy. A simple practice to calm the body and relax is to count the beats when you inhale and exhale naturally, then increase the

[29] Iyengar, B.K.S., *Light on the Yoga Sutras of Patanjali* (California: Harper Collins, 1996), pp. 152-153.

exhalation by two to three counts. This longer out-breath is very calming and nurturing.

And if you choose to energize your body, simply increase the inhalation. First, you count the beats when you inhale and exhale naturally, then increase the inhalation by at least two to three counts of rapid inhaling. These faster, longer breaths are very energizing and often provide a gust of vitality.

As you learn to monitor how you use your energy and focus on how you are breathing, you can become mindful to choose nurturing pursuits and steer away from debilitating activities that deplete energy by *stretching you too far.*

Your Subtle Anatomy Chakra System

"The world belongs to the energetic."

—Ralph Waldo Emerson, American Author

The course of *prana* or life force (also known as ki or chi) flows through a system of chakras or wheels of energy in the body, surrounding your spine, that fan vitality throughout your body. It's important to become aware of these major energy centers that store all of your experiences and affect your demeanor as well as your health. Doreen Virtue, an inspirational author of self-help books and cards, says -- "Your chakras radiate and receive energy constantly. If you hold negative thoughts, your chakras become dirty with dense, dark energy, and you feel sluggish and out of balance." [30]

[30] Virtue, Doreen, *Chakra Clearing* (California: Hay House, 1998), p. viii.

Accordingly, not just your emotions and experiences but also your thoughts affect the energy flow of your chakras.

There are seven main chakras in your body, and each one serves to enhance aliveness and health. Each chakra, located next to a hormonal gland, is responsible for the health of the body's organs surrounding it. Let's take a moment to introduce a quick overview of the chakras and a few suggestions for keeping them vitally alive.

- Starting at the base of your spine is your **Root Chakra,** called ***Muladhara*** in Sanskrit. Located in the anal area, your Root Chakra is responsible for your physical identity, stability, and grounding.
- Your **Second Chakra,** called ***Swadhisthana*** in Sanskrit, is located in your sacral plexus between the gonads or ovaries. The *Swadhisthana* Chakra relates to sex, creativity, finances, and pleasure in living.
- Your **Third Chakra,** called ***Manipura*** (City of Jewels) in Sanskrit, is located just beneath your rib cage in your solar plexus. The *Manipura* Chakra relates to wisdom, clarity, emotions, self-esteem, and confidence.
- At your heart center, your **Fourth Chakra,** called ***Anahata*** in Sanskrit, relates to love, compassion, and acceptance.
- At your throat, your **Fifth Chakra,** called ***Vishuddha*** in Sanskrit, is responsible for willpower, self-expression, and communication.
- On your forehead, just between your eyebrows at your third eye, is your **Sixth Chakra,** called ***Ajna*** in Sanskrit. The *Ajna* Chakra is responsible for your spiritual connection, intuition, and imagination.
- At the crown of your head is your **Seventh Chakra,** called ***Sahasrara*** (1,000 petaled lotus) in Sanskrit. This seventh chakra is your connection to cosmic awareness, Higher Intelligence, and the celestial forces of the Universe.
- Some schools of study, such as Alberto Villoldo's the Four Winds Shamanic Medicine Training, teach about two additional chakras above the head, an eighth chakra connecting energy with the

individual's soul or *Wiracocha* and a ninth chakra of Universal Oneness that is shared by all beings.[31]

- And, according to Dr. Amit Ray, there are 114 prominent chakras, though not active at all times: seven major chakras, twenty-one minor chakras (e.g. in hands, feet, and elbows), and eighty-six micro chakras in the human body.[32]

Just as the pupils of the eyes can be dilated or expanded, similarly, your chakra wheels of energy can be open and flourishing as they spin clockwise. On the other hand, they can be dormant or spinning in the opposite direction if they are blocked.

The chakras seem to gather the residue of the emotional upsets we experience throughout life and need to be cleared often. As I briefly introduce these wheels of energy, I suggest you research how the major chakras work and learn to feel them in your body. Can you recall a time you were upset and felt it in your gut? That happens when an emotional upset affects your solar plexus chakra. Have you ever had the pleasant experience of someone gently patting your back right behind your heart, making you feel really good? This gentle touch may have provided nurturing to your heart chakra.

You can do many activities on your own to nurture your chakras and maintain an open energy flow. Daily exercise, walking, running, dancing, Yoga, Pilates, Reiki, massage, bathing, and a variety of other physical activities help clear blocked chakras and keep your wheels of energy spinning and thriving. Releasing and clearing negative emotions also helps remove the blockage, as does summoning loving thoughts and a higher vibration.

Many healing practitioners work at clearing blocked chakras and restoring full energy flow. When I attended Alberto Villoldo's 300-hour Energy Medicine Training from 2019 to 2021, I learned techniques to scan a client's chakra system and facilitate the removal of blocks in Shamanic

[31] http://www.thefourwinds.com

[32] http://www.amitray.com/72000-nadis-and-114-chakras-in-human-body/

chakra clearing sessions. It's a wonderful experience for me to listen to a client's issues , scan where energy is blocked, and use proven techniques to open up the optimal energy flow.[33]

Know that when you *stretch too far*, it affects not only your mental attitude and level of exhaustion but also the subtle anatomy of your chakra system. Over-extending yourself and enduring emotional setbacks, without clearing them, stifles your health and well-being on so many levels. When time permits, you may want to research the chakra system and learn to apply strategies to boost your subtle anatomy.

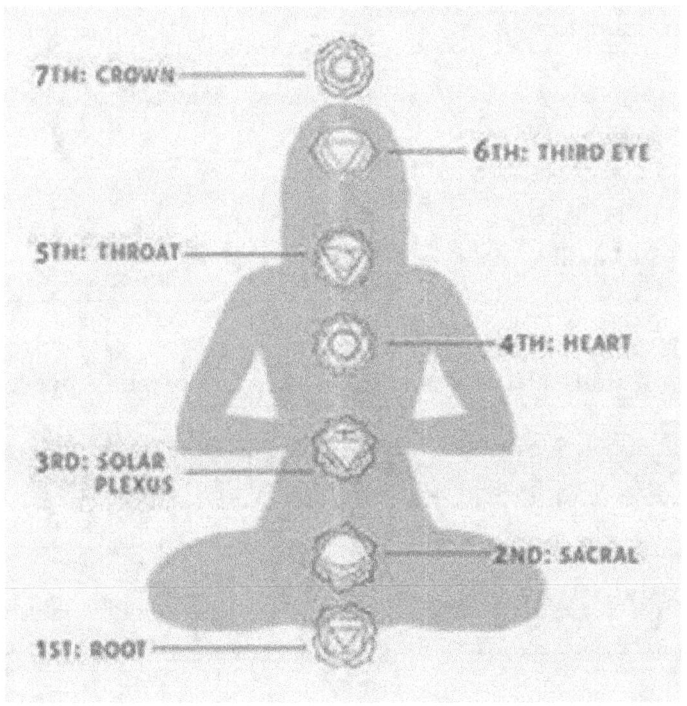

---

[33] http://www.thefourwinds.com

Chakra Chart

Chakra Name	Location	Influences
First Chakra, Muladhara	Base of Spine	Stability and Grounding
Second Chakra, Swadisthana	Sacral Plexus	Sex, Creativity, Finances, Pleasure
Third Chakra, Manipura (Jewel)	Solar Plexus	Emotions, Self-Esteem, Confidence
Fourth Chakra, Anahata	Heart	Love, Compassion, Acceptance
Fifth Chakra, Vishuddha	Throat	Will Power, Self Expression, Communication
Sixth Chakra, Ajna (Third Eye)	Between Eyebrows	Intuition, Imagination, Spiritual Connection
Seventh Chakra, Sahasrara	Crown of Head	Awareness, Intelligence, Celestial
Eighth Chakra, Wiracocha	Above the Head	Soul Essence
Ninth Chakra, Creation	Heart of the Universe	Light Body, Experience of Creation, Highest Chakra Shared by All

Managing How Far You Stretch

"Be moderate in order to taste

the joys of life in abundance."

–Epicurus, Greek Philosopher

Following this principle entails exploring ways you can better manage and nurture your energy. For example, how outgoing and chatty are you in attempts to win over others with your personality? Yes, we can expend energy by being overly talkative and replenish it by being more contained or meditatively silent.

What kinds of activity consume most of your time? In what ways do you tend to squander or dissipate your energy? Do you fritter away countless hours on your cell phone, tablet, computer, or television? Suppose you were to draw an energy pie. How much time do you generally devote to—work, family, friends, community, electronic devices, sports and entertainment, health and hygiene, rest and inactivity, education and self-development? Do you spend any time in uplifting spiritual endeavors and loving service?

First, looking at electronics, are you attached to your cell phone, so much so that if it rings, you interrupt meaningful experiences with people, a meal, or a relaxing bath to answer its call right away or to read and respond to text messages immediately? What electronic devices are you glued to? Are you watching hours of television daily and perhaps binging on those wonderful Netflix seasons of episodes, watching one after the other non-stop? (Mea Culpa!)

How much time do you spend at your computer? Perhaps you are getting too wrapped up in extensive emailing, browsing YouTube, listening to Ted Talks, playing online games, or getting lost in social media such as Facebook, Twitter, TikTok, and Instagram?

What personal pastimes consume inordinate amounts of your energy? Are there any hobbies, sports, spiritual practices, exercise routines, or shopping excursions you may pursue to extremes? I must confess to being a thrift-shopaholic, who cannot resist going into a thrift store for the next great bargain that I do not need. Purchasing is definitely one way I *stretch too far*. How about you?

In what ways are you sometimes excessive in mind, speech, or body? For example, are you ever mentally obsessive about relationships or past or future events? Do you sometimes *stretch too far* with sexual activity, sensual cravings, over-exercising, dessert fetishes, and other physical aspects of life? Think about any areas of excess in your life that you would like to reduce. I invite you to make a plan and set a time frame to compassionately wean yourself of one excess. Set up some reward for yourself when you accomplish the goal, and feel good about yourself for doing so.

Allowing Others to Drain Us Like Sponges

"A man doesn't need brilliance or genius;

all he needs is energy."

—Albert M. Greenfield, Real Estate Developer

What activities and people tend to boost and replenish your life force, and which ones seem to drain your energy? Maybe you are energized by doing physical exercise, spending time out in nature, or being with uplifting teammates and your most loving friends. Perhaps you feel inspired when you attend spiritual activities and community gatherings.

In contrast to these uplifting experiences and persons, notice which actions and people usually exhaust your energy. Perhaps you are depleted by overworking or having to endure complaining colleagues and relatives. Are you able to cut endless phone conversations short when your time is needed elsewhere or you have just heard enough?

Maybe you have difficulty saying "No" when invited to activities that you know are not enriching for you, such as going to a crowded, dimly-lit bar with the gals or guys who generally overdrink or hanging out with old friends in dives that serve food you would rather not eat. How might you sell yourself short at times to gain approval? Are there any projects on your to-do list calling for your attention? How can you minimize vitality drains, nurture your life force, and achieve greater balance by conserving and expending energy in meaningful ways?

Let's Consider Time Sponges

According to late management consultant Peter F. Drucker, "Nothing else, perhaps, distinguishes effective executives as much as their tender loving care of time." In his book *The Effective Executive*, Drucker quotes studies that show how humans have a poor perception of time and are worse at remembering how they spend their time. Drucker says that employees and employers must consider "time sponges" and recognize: things that don't need to be done, things that others could do better, and things that require staff to do work that is not productive.[34]

Think about what might be the time sponges that your team members, family, and associates face and the ways that you may *stretch too far*. What time consuming tasks can you delegate or pay someone to do so that you can enjoy more uplifting free time? What activities take up too

[34] Druker, Peter F., *The Effective Executive: The Definitive Guide to Getting it Right* (New York: Harper Business, 1996).

much of your day and warrant being done more quickly by you or an assistant? Following this principle, a "time sponge" investigation would help you discover ways to diminish energy loss and free up time for more vitalizing activities.

Benefits of Moderation

"To keep a lamp burning we have to keep putting oil in it."

—Mother Theresa, Missionaries of Charity

When we are able to moderate and conserve more life force, the ***Yoga Sutras*** say that great knowledge, vigor, valor, and energy flow to us. Renowned Yoga master, T.K.V. Desikachar, stresses the wisdom of applying this principle to managing our energy field – "At its best, moderation produces the highest individual vitality. Nothing is wanted by us if we seek to develop moderation in all things. Too much of anything results in problems. Too little may be inadequate." [35]

As you can see, there would be more joy in life if everyone could diminish energy depletion and increase nurturing life force. There would be enough energy at day's end to accomplish pleasant things you would like to do. Relationships would improve with more quality time spent with people instead of tackling tiring tasks. And your health would benefit from less drudge and more play. Your life force affects the health of every cell and organ in your body. It affects your attractiveness to others, your personality, your way of living, your relationships, your job performance, and your entire well-being. So, don't waste it!

[35] Desikachar, T.K.V., *Reflections on the Yoga Sutras of Patanjali* (India: Krishnamacharya Yoga Mandarim, 1987), p. 67.

Everyday Lapses in Energy Moderation

Now begin to look into the specific circumstances of your energy expenditure. Skim the following examples of *stretching too far.* See if any of them relate to you. Where might you choose to achieve greater moderation and balance?

- Being too tired at day's end to take care of yourself or your family
- Overeating or over-sleeping to reduce stress
- Indulging in alcohol or drugs to numb yourself
- Spending excess hours absorbed in your cell phone, computer, or television
- Promising yourself to do what's good for you and not following through
- Over-committing your time to others
- Starting a lot of projects and not finishing them
- Having sexual experiences that are less than sacred
- Not heeding the signs when your body is not doing well
- Getting caught in emotional dramas that are draining

Discussion and Journaling for Moderation-- Good Notices, Ahas, Gratitude, Fun Scribbling, Shifts, Intentions, Self-Care

- What does the principle of Moderation suggest to you?
- In what aspects of your everyday life do you practice moderation?
- How do you tend to be excessive in your thoughts, speech or actions?
- Can you think of one way you "overindulge," and create a plan to be more moderate?
- What life experiences seem to drain your energy? Why?
- How can you be more conscious of managing your energy for the highest good?

Ways to Practice Energy Moderation

"The difference between one man and another

is not mere ability—it is energy."

–Thomas Arnold, English Educator and Historian

I will put the principle of Energy Moderation into practice by committing to take the following steps:

- I promise to spend less time absorbed in my cell phone, computer, TV, and other electronic devices that drain energy.
- I will practice moderation in terms of food, alcohol, drugs, caffeine, and sugar.

- I will prioritize activities that nurture my energy, such as exercise, time in nature, and worthwhile projects for the highest good.

Now that you are more focused on curtailing excesses and creating greater balance in your life, you are making progress living Moderation.

Affirmations

- I am in perfect harmony and balance
- I am moderate in my appetites
- I pursue nurturing activities
- I bring good energy to all I meet
- I channel my life force toward the highest good
- I use my energy in Divine service

"Drop In" for Moderation

- Sit in a quiet place and close your eyes
- Breathe into feeling the love in your heart
- Label exterior sensations and let them go
- Nestle into a peaceful, loving place within
- Appreciate yourself for managing your energy for the highest good
- Thank the Universe for the goodness of life

Clinging to nothing
Caressing all in its path
The stream moves forward

CHAPTER FIVE

◇ ◇ ◇

Non-Attachment—
Relax Your Grip

The Fifth *Yama:* The Yoga Principle *APARIGRAHA*, Non-Attachment

Whom or what do you cling to in life?

What do you hold on to too tightly? Could it be your own way of doing things, your favorite possessions, or the people you love most dearly? How often do you do things the same way, as if that's the only way? How flexible are you when it comes to trying new things? Is there anything you cling to in life, even your favorite coffee cup, the car you won't let anyone else drive, or your cell phone and computer? This fifth principle is a calling to *relax your grip*. This Yoga wisdom recommends letting go of attachment to people, preferences, or things. Keep only what you need in the present moment, and trust the Universe to provide more when you need it.

Clinging to people or stockpiling possessions does not bring happiness. It actually alienates people and adds to stress.

A vicious cycle is set in motion when attachments cause desire or longing; this creates suffering. Either people yearn for material things and dependent relationships, or hold on too tightly to their current relationships for fear of losing them.

In both cases, any desire to control people or to amass possessions places attention on what is missing and keeps your energy focused on lack. Since your thoughts create your reality, the more attention you give to what you are wanting, the more energy you are sending to the Universe to keep it lacking.

When you dwell on what's missing, you often succumb to negative emotions of fear, greed, and scarcity instead of shifting your consciousness to being satisfied now, expressing gratitude, and planting seeds for greater abundance.

Let Go of Possessiveness

"The pleasure of modern man is in getting more and more....
But isn't it better to live simply — without so many luxuries and with fewer worries? The time will come when mankind will begin to get away from the consciousness of needing so many material things.
More security and peace will be found in the simple life.

—Paramahansa Yogananda, Indian Yoga Master

Practicing Non-Attachment does not mean that we cannot have nice things. It's just that we relax our hold on the things we do have. It's a matter of not clinging to or hoarding them. We can trust in the flow of spiritual and material abundance. We can allow possessions to come and go without any greed or stockpiling.

By now, I am sure you have heard the story about the monkey who got his hand caught in the jar because he would not let go of the banana. All he had to do was simply let go of the banana, and he could have freed his hand and arm from the jar. Instead, he clung to his object of desire at the expense of his freedom. The point of this story is to look at the "bananas" you may be clinging to at the cost of your freedom.

What are your "bananas"? Are you attached to making something happen that is just not flowing? Are you insisting on certain outcomes instead of allowing things to unfold however they do? Are you accumulating too much clutter? Are you grasping at relationships that could use more space? Are you clinging to friends or perhaps being somewhat controlling with your mate or adult children? Ponder your answers to these questions as you contemplate following this fifth principle of Non-Attachment by *relaxing your grip*.

Trusting in the Flow of Abundance

"What is the world full of? It is full of things that arise, persist, and cease. Grasp and cling to them, and they produce suffering. Don't grasp and cling to them; and they do not produce suffering."

—Buddhadasa, Thai Buddhist Monk

As emphasized earlier, it is important to believe that there is a flow of abundance and to trust life to bring a share of it your way. This is the fundamental belief underlying the principle of non-attachment and *relaxing your grip*. There is no reason to hoard.

Whatever it is that you may be stockpiling, this principle teaches you to take only as much as you can use now, trusting that more will be available when you need it. Just when funds might seem to be getting low, there is often another opportunity coming along if you are open to seeing it. Personally, I plant seeds and trust that I will be taken care of. Sometimes the retreat I have scheduled may not fill, but then a request comes in for a custom group activity or a series of sessions that is even more rewarding. I can recall a time that there were no registrations in a retreat I had scheduled. Despite my disappointment, I had to accept that it was just not happening and refrain from pushing the river.

Shortly thereafter, a call came in from the head of a Chiropractic Professional Association, asking me to choreograph a full day of activities for a group of eighty-five chiropractors attending a conference in Sedona. Wow! We enjoyed a Yoga class indoors at the luxurious L'Auberge de Sedona and a wonderful vortex hike with Yoga and meditation on the red rocks. Needless to say, this was a better gift from the Universe than my little retreat would have been.

Another time, many years earlier, when I was returning from a camping trip in my Ford van, a car backed into me and woke me up as I was sleeping in the van's rear bed. Startled, I got up and had a conversation with the nice older man whose car had hit my van.

He was profusely apologetic as we exchanged license and registration information. He told me to find out the cost of a new bumper so that he could pay for it without involving any insurance companies. The bumper was not horribly dented, but I did find out the cost of a new one and relayed the information to the gentleman the next day. He sent me the money overnight.

Since I could live with the dented bumper, I was relieved to have the Universe send me the money to cover the bills that I was stretching to pay. Denting my van is not how I want the Universe to provide rent money, but it turned out to be a good experience. The point is that the Universe always does provide for me, and I trust that.

Can you trust that the Universe also provides for you? It is truly a matter of faith in the prosperity you attract. It often comes in ways other than those you may have planned. So, the wisdom is to believe that your needs will be provided for, especially in times of apparent scarcity, no matter what it looks like at the time.

How Much Stuff Do You Hoard?

"Be attached to nothing. Be grateful for everything."

—David Che, Author of Total Law of Attraction

This principle of non-greed and non-hoarding sheds light on the need to look at what is really important in life. It helps you look at how you spend your energy and resources in amassing material goods instead of focusing more of that energy on your life's purpose.

The poet Wordsworth pointed this out in his famous line, "Getting and spending, we lay waste our powers. Little we see in nature that is ours." Following this principle, you might explore how much stuff you stockpile. Do you have closets full of seldom-used clothes or shoes? Do you work hard for a paycheck and then spend it on acquiring more possessions? Is your life about getting bigger, better material things, like designer outfits, extravagant houses, or fancy cars?

I must admit that I find it hard to resist a shoe sale and do have a closet full of shoes I rarely wear. Yet, I have started to look at what apparel items I can let go of when I buy new ones. I have a friend who is so into keeping only what she needs that she gives away a coat hanging in her closet when she buys a new jacket or gets rid of a pair of shoes when she buys a new pair. I am not quite as disciplined at minimizing possessions as she is, but I am working at it. How about you?

The late comedian George Carlin has a very famous comedy routine, making fun of how we gather stuff, then need to buy more furniture to hold our stuff, then bigger houses to hold all of the furniture full of stuff, and it goes on and on until we have to write our Last Will and Testaments to let others know what to do with our stuff when we die!

George is so right! I must admit that over the past 70+ years, I have collected a lot of possessions. I cannot resist buying several of the same item when there is a sale or stocking up on packaged food for a rainy day.

Fortunately, I have storage shed space to hold the overflow. So, of all the principles, this is the one I need to address the most. But I have written a Last Will and Testament to tell others what to do with all of my valuable stuff and how to orchestrate my wonderful funeral celebration when I transcend.

What material things do you think will bring you happiness? What is your attitude toward the possessions you already have, the roles you play, and the people you interact with? Can you stretch to trusting that all of your needs will be provided for in the natural flow of abundance? Is it truly necessary for you, me, or any of us to hoard provisions for that proverbial rainy day?

In What Ways Are You Possessive of People?

"Letting go does not mean you stop caring.

It means you stop trying to force others to."

—Mandy Hale, New York Times Best-Selling Author

Turning from material objects to people, let's take a look at our relationships to see where we may be clinging. We might examine ways each of us is sometimes possessive of our relationships, not wanting to share loved ones with others.

Perhaps you have a growing teenage daughter you would like to keep all boys away from, a relationship partner whose whereabouts you would like to monitor all the time, or a favorite pool secretary at the office that you want to work only for you. Recently, I heard a movie character husband tell his wife, "I let you become a nurse, didn't I?" Now there's a perfect example of being controlling in a relationship. It takes a tremendous amount of energy to be possessive and attached. Holding on too tightly sometimes prevents people from seeing the real nature of the person or thing they blindly cleave to. There are far too many people who remain in abusive relationships with people to whom they feel attached.

They just don't allow themselves to see how detrimental these dependent relationships are. The movies, media, and local gossip mills show a wide range of bad things that people do to others who are close to them. There are daily reports of unhealthy behaviors in which people are enablers, stalkers, or abusers, who are verbally and physically violent to alleged loved ones.

It is quite human to want to hold on to what is precious to you. But excess attachment implies that you do not trust your loved ones to behave properly. Perhaps you doubt their values, integrity, and inherent wisdom. It is important to practice loving, appreciating, and trusting others without being controlling. The more you want to control, the less satisfied and contented you are with the blessings of the present moment.

Notice if you are cleaving to a way of doing things at home and at work that is the same way you have always done them, rather than allowing family and teammates to create new policies. This type of clinging is apparent in “Me, My, I” attachments, such as "That's MY cup, MY tablet, MY seat, or MY way of conducting meetings." Take a moment to consider the ways in which you might occasionally be possessive.

I invite you to choose someone or something that you are particularly attached to and see if you can think of one way to reduce your clinging. You might find it valuable to make an inventory of your possessions. List things that are not needed. Jot down how you might sell them or give them away. Take a moment to think about a few new ways that you can lighten up and streamline. I know that I am doing the same.

Personal Experiences with Attachment

I can recall a shift that happened to a friend who insisted on doing everything with her husband. When they were first married, she kept referring to him as “my husband Dave,” even though we all knew him and recognized that he was her husband. I guess she was really glad to be married.

Being somewhat attached, she had always wanted them to play tennis together, even though he was masterful at the game and she was just a struggling beginner. It took a long time for my friend to let go of her possessiveness and send her husband off with her blessings to play tennis with his equals. When she finally did that, she experienced great freedom and joy. My friend had not realized that she was being so possessive, and when she did notice it, she was happy to let it go. It was empowering for both her and her husband when she stopped being joined to his hip.

Several years ago, the house I was living in was on the alert list for evacuation as at least six fires raged across the San Diego area. Some friends, living less than fifteen minutes away, had been evacuated. It was hard to breathe with the windows closed, and when we went outside, we needed to wear face masks or scarves to prevent smoke inhalation.

As I looked at my deck and car covered with ashes and saw the dark clouds of smoke filling the sky, I pondered what I would take with me if the urgent call for immediate evacuation were to be announced. All I could think of was to take the computer hard drive that housed a book I was writing, plus a few special photographs and pieces of jewelry.

People everywhere, from local shopkeepers to evacuated victims, joined forces to help nearby residents. It was a heart-opening revelation to hear everyone share that their material possessions did not matter to them as much as rescuing their neighbors from harm. What was important to us was providing lodging, clothing, and food for the people who had been evacuated. Our focus was on continuing efforts to stop the fire's destruction and to take care of each other and the earth.

Fortunately, my area was not evacuated, and when I was able to open the windows, I was filled with tremendous gratitude for the new fresh air that I had always taken for granted. Yes, I love fine things, but I realize they are not as important as the welfare of fellow beings and the non-material blessings of life.

Benefits of Relaxing Your Grip

"The more you give, the more comes back to you."

—Napoleon Hill, American Self-Help Author

The sages claim that when you are free of greed and possessiveness, you will gain insight into your past and a greater understanding of your personality. B.K.S. Iyengar notes, "When one is steady in living without surplus possessions and greed, one realizes the true meaning of one's life, and all life unfolds before one." [36] Without being pulled by desires to acquire additional possessions, you can more easily discover who you are deep inside and what your life is all about.

Relaxing your grip on the way you want life to be can open you up to receive more of what the Universe has in store for you. Not clinging to people in your life gives them the space to enjoy their own pursuits and then re-discover an uplifting relationship with you. Not holding too tightly to your relationships or possessions gives you the freedom to let people and things come and go as the wheel of life turns.

Refraining from possessiveness is one way that you express your trust in the Universe to provide whatever you need when it is needed. Letting go of control expands your openness to the unexpected delights that life offers you in the present moment.

[36] Iyengar, B.K.S., *Light on the Yoga Sutras of Patanjali* (California: Harper Collins, 1996), p. 144.

Everyday Lapses in Letting Go of Grasping

This is a good opportunity to examine the objects, people, and behaviors you cling to and explore ways to let go and streamline. Take a few moments to review the following examples of unhealthy attachment. See if any apply to you--

- Accumulating unneeded things because they are on sale
- Collecting more clothing and shoes than easily fit in your closet
- Filling a garage or storage unit with items you are unlikely to use
- Being unwilling to part with any of your belongings
- Taking more than your share of anything
- Resisting the suggestions and contributions of others
- Trying to control the outcome of projects you initiate
- Pressuring friends and family to do what you want
- Being jealous of and clinging to people in your life
- Always leading; never following

Discussion and Journaling on Non-Attachment--Good Notices, Ahas, Gratitude, Scribbling, Shifts, Intentions, and Self-Care

- What are your thoughts about the principle of Non-Attachment?
- What type of things do you tend to stockpile or hoard?
- To what people in your life do you feel most possessive? Why?
- How can you release the tendency to insist on having things go your way?
- Where in your life are you clinging to things and people?
- In what ways can you lighten up and streamline?

Ways to Let Go of Grasping

I will put the principle of Non-Attachment into practice by making a commitment to take the following steps:

- I promise to cling less to my favorite friends and companions. I will honor their independence and freedom to follow their hearts, as I follow mine.
- I will cease accumulating surplus purchases. I will take time to clear out stored items in my closet, basement, garage, and storage sheds that are no longer useful to me and recycle them for others.
- I will stay mindful to honor people and be less controlling at home and at work. I vow to stop presenting my way of doing things as the best or only way.

As you free up your grasp to let go of stockpiling possessions and clinging to people, you are succeeding at practicing Non-Attachment.

Affirmations

- I release clinging to people
- I take only what belongs to me
- I let go of collecting more than I need
- I know the Universe always provides for me
- I am content with what is and attached to nothing
  - My life is simple and streamlined

"Drop In" for Non-Attachment

- Sit in a quiet place and close your eyes
- Breathe into feeling the love in your heart
- Label exterior sensations and let them go
- Nestle into a peaceful, loving place within
- Appreciate yourself for letting go of clinging and attachments
- Thank the Universe for the goodness of life

◇ ◇ ◇

From the Yamas to the Niyamas

Reviewing the Yamas or Social Harmony Characteristics

Let's take a few moments to review the first five ancient **Yoga Principles for Social Harmony**—the ***Yamas***. This will help us set the stage for applying the second five codes to achieve greater self-mastery and soulful living—the ***Niyamas***.

- The pinnacle of all ten principles is **Compassion**, and the primary focus is to ***Stay Centered in Your Heart*** with kindness and care for yourself and all beings.
- To live with integrity, it is important to ***Stay Aligned*** with the Truth of who you are. As you practice **Truthfulness,** you are honest and forthright with yourself and everyone else.
- Committed to **Non-Stealing**, you ***Keep Your Eyes on Your Own Mat*** and respect what belongs to others rather than stealing, appropriating, or coveting anything.

- Focusing on **Moderation**, you are mindful to monitor your expenditure of energy for the highest good and ***Not Stretch Too Far*** by overdoing any activity or indulging in draining experiences.
- Lastly, you practice **Non-Attachment** and ***Relax Your Grip*** on your "Me-My-I" way of doing things. You stop clinging to people, projects, and material possessions and do your best to achieve results without being attached to them.

By remembering to practice these five essential human traits, you can create more harmonious relationships with yourself, your family, your colleagues, and your community.

As you achieve social harmony, it is vital to focus on your personal development. What are you doing to heighten your inner state of well-being? How are you enhancing your consciousness these days? What can you do to bring out the best you have to give?

Introducing the Niyamas or Codes for Soulful Living

Ponder these questions as we look at the second set of five ancient Yoga principles, the ***Niyamas***, which are internal observances geared to help you be the most conscious person you can be. Let's look at ways to apply each of the five **Practices for Soulful Living**.

- First, how can you practice greater **Purity** in your life or ***Stay Clean and Focused*** in both your external environment and your internal thoughts?
- As you apply strategies to enhance Purity, how can you create greater **Contentment** in your life? Despite negative challenges, how can you ***Smile into Each Stretch***?

- How can you develop inner **Discipline** in your life and learn to ***Hold the Pose Through Challenges*** amid the ups and downs of life?
- Developing greater discipline helps you focus on **Self-Study** and ***Reflect on Your Practice*** as you live each moment of daily life. You learn to monitor the multitude of decisions you make about your thoughts, actions, and speech as well as your choice of companions, activities, and projects. What can you shift in your everyday behavior to express your best self?
- And this brings us to our supreme principle—**Surrender to a Higher Power**. How can you develop a stronger soul connection with the Intelligence Field of the Universe? How can you be more attentive and receptive to the Divine Forces at play? How can you tap into your core being and learn to ***Trust Inner Guidance***?

Let's examine our five ***Codes for Soulful Living*** and learn how to make a *Soul Stretch* to greater self-mastery and a deeper connection with the Divine.

Radiating peace
Pure in all of its facets
The crystal stays clear

CHAPTER SIX

◇ ◇ ◇

Purity—
Stay Clean and Focused

The First *Niyama:* The Yoga Principle
SHAUCHA, Purity

If you made a commitment to "clean up your life," what would you have to change?

Pondering this question may lead you to examine this first self-mastery principle — Purity or Cleanliness. Do you ever let clutter accumulate until a guest comes over or let your dirty laundry pile up until you have no clean socks? Do you ever speak unkind words about people without thinking? Do you sometimes hold onto bad feelings and resentments?

It is helpful to consider how you might benefit by looking at ways to clean up your mind, heart, body, speech, and environment. To use a slang expression, what can you do to "clean up your act"?

As we aim to do the *Soul Stretch*, we move on to the five core Yoga principles that can help us achieve self-mastery, our five codes to *Practice Soulful Living.* The first principle about developing yourself to the fullest calls for Cleanliness and Purity in body, thought, speech, and action.

The word *Purity* might seem a bit extreme in today's busy world of clutter and back-to-back activities and responsibilities. Personally, I am not sure if my furniture would pass the white glove test, and my mind does seem to want to hold on to negative thoughts sometimes (especially when I know I am right!).

Rather than alluding to any "immaculate" performance, let's look at Purity as a level of higher consciousness to Cleanliness applied to how you live your life, fill your mind, relate to others, and keep your environment. Heightened attention to Purity can help you more fully resonate with whatever experiences life may bring. The purer you are, the more likely you are to be true to yourself, the people in your life, and your higher goals.

In following this principle, you do your best to aim for a high level of Cleanliness and clarity in all aspects of life. And, of course, you must not forget that aspiring to Purity also entails practicing the principles of Compassion and Moderation. While practicing these simultaneously, you are kind to yourself as you aim for greater Cleanliness, and you are conscious to be moderate if you indulge in substances that may not be good for you. You make a commitment to *stay clean and focused.*

Stay Clean and Focused on the Physical Level

"Purity, patience, and perseverance are the three essentials to success and, above all, love."

– Swami Vivekananda, Indian Yoga Master

Obviously, on the physical level, this principle calls you to focus on the Cleanliness of the body in both your home and work environments. Can you immediately think of ways to improve your daily hygiene, your work station, or your clothing closet? Needless to say, to make yourself the best person you can be, it's important to care for your body and keep yourself clean by practicing good hygiene—even when under pressure.

To nurture a healthy, energetic body internally, it is best to practice consciously eating nutritious foods and refrain from ingesting unhealthful substances. When it is "party time," following this principle, you know enough to steer clear of consuming too much of anything that may cause hyperactivity, instability, or lethargy—such as alcohol or sweets. To see how you might upgrade your environment, I invite you to take a look at the state of your car, your living room, your kitchen, and your drawer space. See if there is any way you can organize your home or office space to decrease clutter or grime.

Yes, I know there may be dishes left in the sink occasionally, which can tend to happen at my home too, but the goal is to be attentive to tidiness. Remember, you are aiming to heighten consciousness and improve your life without blaming yourself or others.

In the past, as an assistant to Werner Erhard seminars called "The Forum," I was taught the importance of consciousness to detail when setting up a room for a seminar.

We assistants placed chairs an equal distance apart and put pencils and pads in the exact same position at each seat. We were intent on consciously setting up the room contents and caring for the guests. Whatever opinion you might have about such seminars, they provide a great example of striving for environmental impeccability to produce positive results. Also, conscious Cleanliness does increase comfort, well-being, and an atmosphere conducive to concentration.

Stay Clean and Focused on a Mental Level

"But more important than the physical cleansing of the body is the cleansing of the mind and its disturbing emotions like hatred, passion, anger, lust, greed, delusion, and pride."

– B.K.S. Iyengar, Indian Yoga Master

On a mental level, this principle refers to keeping your mind pure, steady, and free of disturbing emotions. Since the state of the body affects the mind, purifying the body can help you cultivate a peaceful mind. When the body races with caffeine and chocolate, the mind will tend to be quickened and restless. If the mind is numbed with that extra cocktail or glass of wine, that may cloud perception and decision-making.

And then there are the negative thoughts you may allow to enter and stay in your mind. Do you ever entertain critical thoughts of others that may be judgmental personal projections for which you have no actual proof? To keep a pure mind, aim to monitor and process the thoughts you allow your mind to keep. You can recognize and release your ego's judgmental thoughts and not snowball them into big issues that prevent you from being peaceful. You can be mindful not to overindulge by carrying emotions to extreme peaks and valleys. Instead of jumping on that roller coaster ride, see if you can catch yourself becoming upset and deal with your feelings before they escalate. While you do not want to let emotions overpower you, it is important to feel the emotions you are experiencing just as they are, without exaggerating them into greater suffering or denying that they are as gripping as they are. Just as you do not want to add extra, long-lasting drama, you do not want to stuff your feelings or be in denial.

It is best to feel your feelings and release them as quickly as you can rather than indulge yourself in a three-week self-pity party. For example, you can remember not to get carried away with uncontrollable excitement when life gives you unexpected good fortune. You can also remind yourself not to plunge into deep despair when something disappointing happens. Remember to recite that wonderful mantra: "This too shall pass." Moments of joy are to be totally savored, and disappointments are to be felt, cleared, and learned from.

Practicing Purity of mind, body, and spirit, you strive to stay balanced and centered through both joy and sadness, feeling your emotions and releasing them. Refraining from adding extra soap-opera drama to events that happen, you aim to keep your mind clear and unclouded by distractions.

Practicing Purity Is Looking at Why You Think, Say, and Do What You Do

"My strength is as the strength of ten because my heart is pure."

– Alfred Lord Tennyson, British Poet Laureate

This principle of Purity calls for you to examine your motives and ponder why you think, say, and do what you do. You are not entirely focused or genuinely present when you have hidden motives or agendas. Yet, when your heart is pure, you can be fully present and clear in your actions and interactions. Being pure enables you to be open and authentic.

It's helpful to examine your mind to see if you may be operating from any agendas for personal gain when you offer to help others. Did you purposely apply that extra effort to help a colleague in order to gain points with the boss? Were you helping your neighbor carry boxes because you wanted to borrow his ladder again? One way to promote a clean mind is to examine and acknowledge the motivation for your thoughts, words, and actions. Having an agenda is okay as long as you are honest about it.

Applying Purity to speech entails thinking before speaking and contemplating how your words may affect others. Practice being truly aware of what you say. From a pure heart, care how your words may affect others; do your best not to say damaging things or gossip about people, and remember to practice our paramount principle of Compassion. If you find fault with someone's behavior, you can step back from criticizing and move away gracefully.

Be a Self-Cleaning Oven

"Think positively about yourself, keep your thoughts
and your actions clean, ask God, who made you,
to keep on remaking you."

– Norman Vincent Peale, Minister and Author

A metaphor I like to use is that caring for ourselves is being a "Self-Cleaning Oven." This principle of Purity, like all the other principles, is about heightening consciousness of what's happening in your mind, body, relationships, and every other area in your life. It is important to discern what is going on inside you that belongs to you and what you may have picked up from other sources.

Sometimes what you feel does not originate from within you but is taken from someone else. Just as the oven gets splashed with grease and covered with gunk, you may pick up feelings from the people and environments you encounter that can negatively affect your energy. For example, you might feel annoyed after someone dumps whining complaints on you and find that you have picked up some of that person's irritability. Or, you may spend time in a shopping mall with glaring fluorescent lights and feel frenzied energy from that lighting.

Have you ever stopped in a new restaurant and left immediately because the vibe did not feel right? This abrupt restaurant turnabout is an example of honing in on the surrounding environment and refraining from picking up its negativity. It is good to recognize when your energy is being negatively affected and do whatever you can to clear yourself.

There are numerous ways to clear energy, such as taking a shower, applying aromatherapy oils, doing a breathing exercise, listening to soothing music, writing in a journal, going for a walk out in nature, or taking a brief time-out to sit still, meditate, do yoga, or lie down. The key is to recognize the presence of negativity, then pause whatever you are doing, find a way to release the uncomfortable energy, and shift consciousness.

As I mentioned earlier in our chapter on Truthfulness, when we find ourselves having trouble letting go of past painful experiences, there may be something we are not telling the full truth about or something we need to forgive ourselves or others for. If past hurts tend to plague you, see if you can clean them up by telling the truth about your role in these experiences and forgiving yourself and the others involved.

Sometimes when I am debriefing the retreats I lead, I have to examine guest challenges that may have arisen during a week's activities. I re-run the series of activities surrounding any guest's upset to examine how events occurred and, particularly, my role in relating to the guest.

Usually, as I look in retrospect at how I may have handled a situation, I see what I would choose to do differently and admit that to myself—without blame. Once I tell myself the truth about something I did or did not do that a guest may have found displeasing, it lightens up for me. I can then choose to do things differently the next time, forgive myself and the challenging guest, and bless us all. The saying "The truth shall set you free" is worth repeating here.

Instead of carrying the heavy baggage of accumulated past hurts, you can explore and purge these issues to keep your energy clear and flowing and your heart open. Once you know that each of us is an energy body, it becomes your job to *stay clean and focused*, balanced, and centered. Once you clear yourself like a self-cleaning oven, you can do your best to fill your "bucket" with positive feelings as discussed earlier.

One of the best ways to be a self-cleaning oven is to learn to use kinesiology to muscle-test if your beliefs are actually empowering. Following Bruce Lipton's recommendation, I became trained as a PSYCH-K® facilitator and learned processes to examine beliefs that are limiting and shift them to more positive ones using muscle-testing and follow-up balancing procedures. Once a belief tests weak, the PSYCH-K® process enables you to permanently shift the disempowering belief to one that is more supportive. I have learned to do this with my clients and myself with instant success, shifting our limiting beliefs about various subjects such as career decisions, personal goals, relationships, money, and health. You can learn more about how to create these miraculous belief shifts in your life at PSYCH-K®.com.

Practice the Four D's for Transforming Upsets

Sometimes when the intention to clear or release an upset does not work, a good strategy is to recreate what happened and examine it in a different context to see if you can transform the experience. If the energy disruption is emotional, I recommend a series of steps that I have named the Four D's for Transformation. The 4D process suggests that you focus on four strategies to clear emotional upsets and return to feeling good. When you notice (Distinguish) something that you would like to shift, be grateful that it has come to your awareness. Otherwise, it might have festered inside you, creating more problems. You can begin practicing the Four D's:

- **Distinguish** the problem and feel its effects
- **Detach** from it (Gain a bit of distance)
- **Dip** the incident in Forgiveness, Gratitude, and Humor (F.G.H.)
- **Design** a more appealing outcome and experience it fully

Four D's: Distinguish, Detach, Dip & Design

- **Distinguish It**: As you become accustomed to living from a calm and centered place, notice when anything upsets your peace of mind. Focus on the present moment and whatever is currently disturbing your serenity. Get in touch with it. Describe it and how it makes you feel. Consciously allow it to be there. Give it your permission. Fully experience it in your mind and heart, and with all five senses of your body.

- **Detach from It**: See if you can get some distance from the issue. Perhaps gain some physical distance by leaving the room and going somewhere outside. Find something else to focus your attention on for a while, even if it's doing the dishes or washing the car. Do your best to move away from negative feelings as you aim to shrink the importance of whatever disturbed you earlier. Shift to being as neutral as you can about it. Tell yourself that you can "let it go for now." Recite the comforting mantra, "This too shall pass." Sometimes, I put the issue on a subway train and watch the doors close as the train leaves the station. Do whatever works for you to gain some distance from the upset.

- **Dip It in Forgiveness, Gratitude, and Humor (F.G.H.)**: The triple dip has you first look at FORGIVENESS. See if you can find it in your heart to look at the situation from the other person's point of view and forgive him or her for whatever happened. It is most important to make sure that you forgive yourself for your involvement in the issue. Then move on to GRATITUDE and ponder the "silver lining." Find something to be grateful for. Think about the nature of the situation in a more positive light that makes you feel better and lighten up. Ask yourself, "What good can come from this?" Lastly, see if you can dip it in HUMOR. Perhaps you can exaggerate what happened to the point of finding it funny and laughable. It really lightens up life when you can make fun of yourself and laugh at your perceived blunders. *(Note: A good way to remember the three dips is to think of the order of the letters in the alphabet F…G…H… for Forgiveness…Gratitude…Humor.)*

- **Design a New Outcome**: After lightening up with a bit of Forgiveness, Gratitude, and Humor, create a new movie scene that pictures the way you want the situation to be in your mind's eye. Design it with vivid sensory detail so you can see, feel, touch, taste, and hear it. Consider your preferred outcome already accomplished. Visualize and feel it. Savor it throughout your being as you experience it fully. Hopefully, following this process of Four D's will help you lighten up any issue.

Personal Example of Using the Four D's

A funny personal example of using the Four D's occurred in my late 20s. A guy I had been dating for months broke up with me over what seemed a stupid disagreement to me but a deal breaker to him. Of course, I apologized and tried everything to change his mind, but to no avail. Finally, I had to accept the loss of someone I really liked and "get over it!" At that time, I was attending a seminar that dealt with using humor to enhance everyday life. And that is just what I did.

Practicing the Four D's, I DISTINGUISHED my upset and despair and let myself feel the sadness of losing him for a while, recalling the things we used to love to do together. Allowing myself to distinguish and feel my sorrow gave it permission to be there, and it soon started to lessen. Then, I took a break from feeling bad about it, and turned on the TV, where I found an old western movie to watch and forget him for a while. I DETACHED from it and gave was able to put it out of my mind. After getting a little distance from the breakup, I DIPPED "him" in FORGIVENESS for breaking up with me, felt GRATITUDE for the good times we did have, and turned to HUMOR—creating a western country scene of my own. I imagined that he and I were out west at a train station. I saw myself wearing an old western country bustle gown and bonnet, saying farewell to him in his cowboy outfit and boots as we waited for his train.

Crying out to him with love, I fell to the ground, grabbing his cowboy boot ankle, pleading with him not to leave me, repeating, "Please don't leave me. I love you. I don't want to live without you!" Unmoved by my cries, he broke loose from my grip and boarded the train. Utterly forlorn, I jumped onto the railroad tracks just as his train began moving, ending it all! After taking my heartache to the height of the western heroine's refusal to live any longer, my distress completely diminished, and I found myself laughing at the extreme exaggeration.

Next, I DESIGNED in my mind the type of wonderful relationship I would soon manifest with the future man of my dreams. I could see my new beau's handsome face and gentle nature as he held me lovingly in his arms. I envisioned us sharing dinners, red rock hikes, beach walks, and traveling to sacred sites around the world. Then, I smiled, feeling that we were the happiest couple ever!

So ends my Four D's example. I personally hope you will try the technique of humorous exaggeration to lighten up whatever troubles you.

To transform any upset, you can start by becoming accustomed to monitoring your feelings. Discover whatever the feel-good, at peace, contentment zone is for you and create the intention to stay in that "bucket-full" place. Maintain an optimal sense of well-being (pure mind and emotions) as your natural state. *Stay clean and focused.*

When you are centered in your core consciousness and fully grounded, you are open for joy to flow through you. If something causes a shift that pulls you away from feeling good, identify the disturbing emotion, stop whatever you have been doing, and take steps to clear it.

See if you can use the Distinguish-Detach-Dip-and-Design 4 D's to lighten up and return to your optimal feel-good state. To follow this principle of Purity, use any of the tools mentioned here or the many ways you already know to practice stopping negativity and shifting to higher consciousness.

Benefits of Practicing Purity – Staying Clean and Focused

"When the body is cleansed, the mind purified, and the sensed controlled, joyful awareness needed to realize the inner self also comes. With cleanliness, the body becomes the temple of the seer and feels the joy of self-awareness. When the consciousness is cheerful and benevolent, the seeker becomes ready to receive the knowledge and vision of the soul."

– B.K.S. Iyengar, Indian Yoga Master

According to ***The Yoga Sutras***, the reward for Purity is that when the body is cleansed, the mind purified, and the senses subdued, we can experience the joy of our inner being. Purity, the sutras say, brings greater clarity and receptivity to life's messages in each moment. As you master Purity, you become more acutely aware of your senses, better able to focus your attention, clearer and more expansive in your perceptions.

You are then able to access inner joy and learn more about your Higher Self or core consciousness. Swami Satchidananda notes that when you master Cleanliness, you gain the Purity of being: "cheerfulness of mind, one-pointedness, mastery over the senses, and fitness for Self-realization."[37]

Once any emotional baggage has been cleansed, your attention can move inward to reflect on the profound nature of who you truly are. Purity makes it possible for you to pursue knowing your spiritual nature and life purpose. In refining your body, thoughts, and emotions, you are able to access the joy within and radiate that inner spirit.

[37] Satchidananda, Sri Swami, *The Yoga Sutras of Patanjali* (Virginia: Integral Yoga Publications, 1978), pp. 142-143).

Everyday Lapses in Purity

"Unless you have a great deal of Purity,

it's difficult to retain the higher Light."

– Frederick Lenz, American Author

Here are several common examples of ways people may need to address greater Cleanliness and Purity. See if any of them apply to you-

- A messy car with scattered junk on the floor and seats
- An office desk with too much clutter to find things
- A body and mind numbed by alcohol or other substances
- Inability to concentrate due to disturbing thoughts
- Recycling, snowballing, and projecting negative emotions
- Going for periods of time without feeling peace and balance within
- Neglecting to take care of your body and surroundings properly
- Doing a favor only because you want to get something in return
- Having negative or impure thoughts about a colleague or neighbor
- Keeping your mind glued to cell phone, TV, and computer screens

Discussion and Journal Writing on Purity – Good Notices, Ahas, Gratitude, Fun Scribbling, Shifts, Intentions, and Self-Care

- What are your first impressions of the principle of Purity and Cleanliness?
- In what facets of your life are you meticulous about purity and neatness?
- How can you pay more attention to positive thinking and tidiness?
- How might you upgrade your physical hygiene, diet, or surroundings?
- What negative thoughts or agendas might you have that you would like to transform?
- Is there anything you can do to deepen your practice of purity and cleanliness?

Ways to Apply the Principle of Purity -- Stay Clean and Focused

I will practice greater Purity by choosing to take the following steps:

- Starting now, I will focus on cleaning up any clutter in my car, office, home, and garage. Gradually and mindfully, I will clean and organize my various environments to support comfort, well-being, and productivity.
- I will consider the potential impact my words might have on others before speaking. I will make sure to be conscious of what I think and say and refrain from criticism and gossip.

- To upgrade the Purity of my body, I will be more conscious that what I eat and drink is good for my health. I will redouble my efforts to wean myself of any addictions and prioritize daily personal hygiene and environmental tidiness.

If you now see how you can achieve greater Cleanliness and Purity in your life, you are successfully implementing this principle

Affirmations

- My heart is pure
- My mind is clear and one-pointed
- My environment is neat and clean
- My body is fully cleansed
- I eat consciously
- I am filled with Divine energy

"Drop In" for Purity

- Sit in a quiet place and close your eyes
- Breathe into feeling the love in your heart
- Label exterior sensations and let them go
- Nestle into a peaceful, loving place within
- Appreciate yourself for your pure heart and cleanliness
- Thank the Universe for the goodness of life

Santosha

Basking in the sun
Gazing beyond the soil below
The sunflower looks up

CHAPTER SEVEN

◇ ◇ ◇

Contentment—
Smile into Each Stretch

The Second *Niyama:* The Yoga Principle
SANTOSHA, Contentment

How much of the time are you content, and
what undermines your joy the rest of the time?

"Nobody can bring you peace but yourself."

—Ralph Waldo Emmerson, American Philosopher

We all know the old expression about turning lemons into lemonade. In medieval chemistry, there were alchemists who practiced turning base metals into gold, a wonderful concept for enriching abundance. You, too, can become an alchemist. You can learn to practice your own form of alchemy as you turn life's less-than-great moments into valuable experiences. No matter what happens in life, all circumstances are transitory and seen through each individual's subjective viewpoint.

Nothing is by nature "negative." The negativity exists only in your perceptions. Since all perceptions are created by the mind, why not mine for gold and turn unappreciated occurrences into golden moments?

As an alchemist, you can also look for the "silver lining" and possible benefits in everything that occurs. In Earth School, everything that happens is here to teach lessons and is beneficial in that respect.

Every moment you have lived has unfolded exactly as it was meant to. It is all perfect in the scheme of life. All events lead to new decisions and new directions. You can learn to turn the pennies of life into solid gold just by shifting your awareness.

The Wisdom of Non-Attachment to Outcomes: Being Satisfied with Whatever Happens

"You know why it's hard to be happy—it's because we refuse to Let Go of thinks that make us sad."

—Bruce H. Lipton, Developmental Biologist

The second personal development principle of soulful living is to cultivate Contentment and good-heartedness. This precept, called *Santosha* in Sanskrit, urges you to be willing to accept whatever fate may bring with balance, gratitude, and joy. It encourages you to detach from your daily experience and become an objective witness, observing yourself on a transcendent level.

By practicing Contentment, you can learn to be an impartial spectator, sitting in the stands and viewing yourself playing out your life on the stage. As a witness, you can remain unattached to achieving your desired outcomes. You can learn to tell yourself to be satisfied with whatever is happening, just for now.

Practicing Contentment does not mean that you never experience dissatisfaction with circumstances. You are simply willing to make the most of any situation. It does not guarantee that you will never get frustrated or emotionally upset. When life does throw you off balance, staying true to your commitment to be content allows you to focus on the positive and get back on track. You learn to *smile into each stretch* that life brings.

In addition to applying this Contentment to your personal life, you express good-heartedness and benevolence to others as well, allowing people to be as they are without judgment. It is helpful to develop a constant awareness and vigilance over judging, which is one of the automatic mind's favorite pastimes. As mentioned earlier, saying "Good notice!" and shifting from judging to kindness are great practices to develop as you pursue becoming more compassionate and content.

When you are feeling out of harmony with life, you can practice Contentment by taking steps to center yourself and accept whatever has happened and how it makes you feel. Then find a way to be okay with it for the time being. You can be grateful that what is happening may point to the need for change. When challenging things happen, you must accept them before anything can lighten up. And, in severely troubling times, it might be good to seek professional help.

The Yoga Sutras teach that suffering is the pain you add when you do not like what is happening. The teaching is that you do not have to suffer. In Part II, Sutra #16 states, "But the suffering yet to come should be averted."[38] Adding dramatic suffering is a matter of choice.

While everyone does have to experience some pain or grief as the wheel of life rolls around, you do not have to create additional misery by magnifying negativity and adding emotional trauma. In the ultimate practice of Contentment, you maintain serenity in the presence of life's ups and downs. You can learn to view the apparent "breakdowns" as messages from the Universe that a needed "breakthrough" is at hand.

Yes, you do need to feel whatever emotions may be present in order to release them, but you do not need to dwell on what's not working well. You can learn to see pain and pleasure, hardship and ease, through the eyes of unconditional love, without succumbing to extreme emotional disturbance. According to this principle, when you master Contentment, you will be supremely happy and totally free of desires and attachments.

[38] Shearer, Alistair, *The Yoga Sutras of Patanjali* (New York: Bell Tower, 1982), p. 105.

Turn Issues into Blessings

"Trade your expectation for appreciation

and your world changes instantly."

—Tony Robbins, Motivational Speaker and Author

Instead of turning perceptions into issues, we can choose to turn them into blessings. You can make a commitment to simply let go of any negative thoughts and focus on being grateful.

You can avoid turning yourself into a victim, like a wife who still complains about her husband who left her ten years ago. No matter what happens, you can do your best to maintain emotional serenity.

If you happen to get caught in deep emotions, you can feel them, then free yourself from them as soon as possible, so you can return to a peaceful state. You can be mindful and trust in the flow of events, believing that everything that occurs is ultimately for the highest good of all. As Deepak Chopra says, "Every problem is an opportunity in disguise." Sometimes a person is fired from a job because there is a more rewarding one coming. Someone may lose a partner because there is one who is a more perfect match about to show up. You might miss a train because you are supposed to meet someone.

If you review your life experience, you will probably think of several events that seemed negative at the time but later presented favorable opportunities. Seeing the blessings comes after feeling the initial emotions and allowing them to be there. As noted earlier, it is not healthy to stuff or deny emotions and cover them up with positive thinking.

A rather crude metaphor for this would be "putting on perfume to cover up body odor." It just does not work! It is always beneficial to feel your genuine emotions so that you can first have the feelings and then release them.

From a place of peace and renewed clarity, you can ask the question, "Why is this happening?" Perhaps some insights will appear if you do not get caught in the drama.

Being Contented Means Loving Yourself Unconditionally

"To be contented is to be good friends with yourself."

–Bliss Carman, Canadian Poet

While most of us associate Contentment with the need to accept and be satisfied with whatever life throws at us, the core of Contentment is internal. Contentment lives inside each of us as self-love. When you love yourself unconditionally, you are strong enough to ride out the vicissitudes of life. It is critical to maintain and nurture your self-esteem and feel good about yourself no matter what life may bring.

In my business, *Sedona Spirit Yoga, Healings, and Vortex Journeys*, I help clients get in touch with their inner strength and build self-esteem when confronted with life's challenges. Sometimes, in my home studio, I do Shamanic chakra-clearing sessions that begin with clients sharing troubling emotions they choose to release.

Out amid Sedona's red rocks, I lead vortex Yoga journeys that include gentle hiking, optional Yoga, meditation, and life coaching. During these vortex journeys, it's not so much about mastering Yoga poses as it is about communing with nature and using the vortex energy to clear past experiences and set intentions. These nurturing events provide the opportunity for intimate sharing, energy clearing, and a shift toward greater Contentment.

Recently, I have been leading vortex journeys for families with teenagers. I like to make it a priority to walk with each young person separately to hear about their concerns. Often, they tell me about what they would like to shift in their lives. I recall two attractive female teens, who told me they were very unhappy. They readily confided in me that they did not think they were pretty enough to attract boys like some of the other girls. As I asked why they felt this way, they revealed they were not as attractive as the girls they were seeing on social media and in some of their school classes.

What was I to say? I always trust that the Universe will guide me. I shared my perceptions and made sure to compliment each one in turn privately, walking beside one girl and then her friend, as we all enjoyed the winding red rock scenery. I tried to help them both shift to seeing their genuine assets (e.g., great eyes, a good figure, very bright, lovely personality). I talked to each one about the idea that if we do not love ourselves—just as we are or are not—who will? I shared with them that having self-esteem is a vital part of living a good life.

After our uplifting chats, the teens expressed new willingness to explore liking themselves. I requested they take on finding ways to be more content with themselves and their young lives. I invited them to think about reasons they had to be grateful. They liked my suggestion that they spend time together helping each other feel good about parts of themselves they formerly complained about, perhaps do some journal writing to release their discontented feelings, and make a gratitude list of the blessings in each of their lives.

It's good that schools are focusing on reducing widespread bullying, but there needs to be a way for schools to help families counter the negative effects of social media and teach youngsters values like self-acceptance, self-esteem, and Contentment. You might choose to start by asking your children or young relatives to share with you how they feel about themselves.

And you can definitely also ask yourself how you feel about your appearance, personality, career, and relationships. How contented are you these days, and what might you choose to shift? Are there parts of yourself that you do not love and want to change? How can you practice greater self-acceptance and love yourself more fully? Being at peace with external circumstances starts with being internally content with yourself.

"To fall in love with yourself

is the first secret to happiness."

—Robert Morley, English Actor

The most important way to practice Contentment is to learn to be satisfied with yourself, your looks, your personality, your career, and your way of being and doing things. For decades, I grimaced whenever I looked in the mirror and disliked that my thighs bulged out of my petite body. I don't recall what seminar experience precipitated it, but there was some exercise about trading parts of our bodies within a small group.

After trading my bulging thighs, I started to let go of belittling myself about them. At some point thereafter, I just accepted that my body was attractive, even with its somewhat bulging thighs. Quite a breakthrough! Now, how about you? What belittling conversations about yourself might you recognize and shift?

How Can We Cultivate Contentment When Bad Things Happen?

"Every adversity, every failure, every heartache carries with it the seed of equal or greater benefit."

–Napoleon Hill, American Self-Help Author

There are times in life when it is very challenging, if not impossible, to be okay with what has happened in the world or in your personal life. A loved one's death, a terminal disease diagnosis, a divorce sought by your beloved partner, learning that your infant child has a lifelong physical ailment, and discovering a family member has committed suicide are some horrors of life that make Contentment seem unfathomable. Personally, I recall the devastating loss I felt when I learned that my mother had died. There was no easy summoning of Contentment. I had to feel the pain, feel the loss, and deal with not having her presence in my life. But my family and I did get through it being grateful that Mom was no longer suffering and by treasuring all the blessings of her love.

Since the pandemic began, I have been leading customized vortex Yoga and meditation journeys for many families undergoing stress—a memorial for a teen who committed suicide, a clearing for a woman who was intent on releasing sexual abuse, and a renewal for a mother whose six-year-old had been diagnosed with a life-long illness.

What I have found most helpful is listening and allowing clients to speak about what they are thinking and feeling. Somehow, once your concerns are really heard and faced, they start to lighten up. After pent up emotions are released, there is an opening to see the blessings for which one has to be grateful. Of course, quieting the mind with Yoga and meditation helps.

So, what are you to do when life brings such tragedy? Following all ten principles, you stay aligned with the Truth of what is, what it makes you feel, and what actions are best to take—and you pray that the Universe is sending you the resources you need. Tap into that prayerful connection to Spirit to give you strength and do your best to feel the wonderful gratitude that turns gripes into grace.

Create Contentment One Decision at a Time: Decide to Be Okay with Whatever Happens

"Start your day with good intentions and set yourself up for a good attitude. It's not what happens to you that matters but how you respond."

—Ken Blanchard, American Business Consultant

Contentment is achieved one decision at a time. To pursue ongoing Contentment, make a decision to love yourself (regardless of any moods), appreciate your appearance, respect your achievements, and admire your own personality and way of being—just the way you are or are not. When you wake up in the morning, you can decide to be good-natured. You can make a commitment to be satisfied with yourself and whatever your day might bring. You can make a decision to *smile into each stretch* or challenge that the day might bring.

I, personally, am not a smiling, "Sunshine Sally," type of person. Yet, in my heart, I am truly grateful for every part of my life. However, I do have to watch out for potholes that I can so easily step into. One of these potholes is the tendency to get "too intense" about things. Each day I pray that I may respond to whatever life sends me with grace and ease. Some days, I experience more grace and ease than others, but it is always the goal.

And while I might be briefly throttled by life's tribulations, I am committed to feeling them and processing them quickly. In this way, I cultivate Contentment on a daily basis. I have come to realize that being content means being "in accord" or "okay with" whatever happens. We need to surrender our likes and dislikes to achieve harmony with ourselves and others in life.

Making Things "Temporarily Okay"

"Success is getting what you want.

Happiness is wanting what you get."

–Dale Carnegie, Self-Improvement Author

I can recall tossing and turning, unable to sleep, with a noisy group of drinkers partying in the Sedona campsite adjacent to mine. I lay awake, saying to myself, "I can be okay with this." After a while, I did not even hear them. Before learning to put harmony first, I might have become angry at the noisy campers or gotten up to politely ask them to be quiet. Instead, I just accepted what was happening and let myself take a moment to be okay with it. When you find yourself out of sync with events, you might use the Four D's discussed in the previous chapter to get back on track. Remember to Distinguish the upsetting emotions, Detach from them, Dip the incident in Forgiveness, Gratitude, and Humor, and Design your preferred outcome.

When you make a commitment to be content, you are deciding to be good-natured and harmonious with everyone and everything. That does not mean you agree with everything or everyone, but that you are able to recognize what is happening and align your energy to be satisfied with it for the time being. Yes, you may be facing real difficulties, but as Tony Robbins reminds us -- "The only people without problems are those in cemeteries." Making things "temporarily okay" helps you to regain the peace and calm to look into what change might be needed.

When you make peace with whatever happens, you are more attentive to reap the value of the messages that everything brings, especially what they teach you about yourself. Instead of seeing the proverbial half empty glass, you can intentionally focus on the half full one. You can become the alchemist who transforms the worst situation into a reason to celebrate! You truly can *smile into each stretch* on the Yoga mat of life!

Benefits of Practicing Contentment

"Contentment ... [is] the ability to be comfortable with what we have and what we do not have.

—T.K.V. Desikachar, Indian Yoga Master

Patanjali's Yoga Sutras say that by practicing Contentment and good-heartedness, we can attain supreme happiness.[39] No matter what happens, you can bring satisfaction to your life by expressing ongoing gratitude. When you are content with yourself and your life, you are more open-hearted and good-natured toward others. You can dwell on appreciating what you have instead of lamenting what you do not have.

[39] Satchidananda, Sri Swami, *The Yoga Sutras of Patanjali* (Virginia: Integral Yoga Publications, 1978), pp. 146).

Instead of identifying with experiences outside of yourself, you can appreciate and identify with the core essence or Divine Light of your inner being. Practicing Contentment helps you accept reality and not resist what is so. Being at peace with life helps you stay present to what is happening in the moment and open to receive life's messages. Focusing on Contentment helps you to accept yourself more and create more meaningful relationships with others. When you are content with yourself, you have more love to share.

Examples of Lapses in Contentment

Here are several examples of ways people tend to be less than content with life. See if any of them apply to you

- Complaining about your lot in life
- Telling the same bad experience to bunches of people
- Thinking — "When am I ever going to get a break?!"
- Focusing on what you do not have instead of what you have
- Being unhappy with yourself for things you have or haven't done
- Carrying longtime grudges and resentments
- Feeling unlucky at love, cards, or anything
- Thinking if that one thing happened, then you would be happy
- Blaming others in your life for your discontent
- Not trusting that life's flow of abundance will reach you

Discussion and Journaling on Contentment--Good Notices, Ahas, Gratitude, Fun Scribbling, Shifts, Intentions, Self-Care

- What insights do you have about the principle of Contentment?
- How much of the time are you contented with yourself and your life?
- What circumstances prompt you to lose that positive feeling of contentment?
- Are there occurrences in your life that tend to get you hooked (i.e. emotionally disturbed)?
- What can you do to stay centered and grateful amid negative circumstances?

Ways to Apply Contentment in Daily Life

To increase ongoing Contentment in my life, I will focus on the following:

- I will make a commitment each day to welcome what life brings and find ways to plant seeds to shift whatever may be displeasing.
- I promise to notice when I am discontented and find ways to be "temporarily okay" with whatever is happening that I do not like.
- When clouds come, I will always look for the "silver lining" and the rainbows on the horizon.

If you are feeling greater satisfaction with your life exactly as it is, you are already building Contentment within.

Affirmations

- I am contented with myself and my life
- I am grateful for everything that happens to me
- I maintain my balance in the face of hardships
- I rejoice in the flow of life
- I see God's goodness everywhere
- I am a lighthearted being

"Drop In" for Contentment

- Sit in a quiet place and close your eyes
- Breathe into feeling the love in your heart
- Label exterior sensations and let them go
- Nestle into a peaceful, loving place within
- Appreciate yourself for being contented with whatever life brings
- Thank the Universe for the goodness of life

Consuming desires
Keenly focused on target
The burning arrow prevails

CHAPTER EIGHT

◇ ◇ ◇

Discipline—
Hold the Pose through Challenges

The Third *Niyama:* The Yoga Principle *TAPAS*, Discipline

In what areas of your life would you like to have greater Discipline?

What pictures does the word "Discipline" evoke in your mind's eye? Does it conjure images of helpless, teary-eyed youngsters with their hands being smacked hard by a schoolmaster's ruler or their buttocks being whipped to redness by an angry father's belt strap? Sadly, for many people, the word Discipline may evoke images of punishing others or being punished by them or chastised for things they did or did not do.

In contrast, your pictures of Discipline may have conjured images of the list of things you have wanted the power to achieve. Perhaps you saw yourself having the strength to lose that excess ten pounds, stick to that exercise routine, or actually read the many books you have accumulated.

For some, the word Discipline may summon pictures of military rigor or required behavior that trainers require of athletes and ballerinas to achieve success. Sometimes the Discipline structure from the outside is agreed upon as part of entering an educational program, adopting a volunteer role in the community, or accepting a job at work.

In most cases, the structure of Discipline imposed from the outside has to be met with internal self-control to fulfill requirements and expectations. It helps to remember to summon the rigor or Discipline needed to make life run smoothly. For example, if the imposed speed limit is 65 mph, you must adhere to that or possibly suffer consequences.

Take a look at the facets of Discipline operating in your life. Notice instances in which you must follow the external rules imposed by authorities at work, home, or in society, as well as personal situations requiring that you exert self-discipline. What do you notice? On a scale of 1-10, how disciplined would you say you are in your life?

Discipline as Self-Love and Personal Rigor

"Patience, persistence, and perspiration make an unbelievable combination for success."

– Napoleon Hill, American Self-Help Author

Discipline has gotten "a bad rap!" It has the connotation of an authority figure chastising you or doing whatever it takes to whip you into shape.

There is a great difference between Discipline inflicted on you from the outside, which can be a form of safety, training, control, punishment, or manipulation, and Discipline from the inside, which is a form of nurturing self-love.

In reality, self-discipline is a good thing. It's about having the strength to do what is needed to bring out your best.

Having Discipline means you are compassionately rigorous with yourself. In a wholesome way, you push yourself to achieve your goals and do what is beneficial for your body, mind, spirit, and all of your roles and relationships.

You are treating yourself well when you develop self-restraint over the many distractions that can pull you away from accomplishing your goals.

Practicing Discipline helps you achieve mental strength and control over your body, mind, and speech that is beneficial to you and others. Being Disciplined is a way of loving yourself and bringing out your best. You are rigorous with yourself because you care about the life you are creating and how you show up in the world. In what areas of your life would you like to have greater Discipline?

Applying the Wisdom of Discipline

"Persistence overshadows even talent as the most valuable resource shaping the quality of life."

– Tony Robbins, Motivational Speaker and Author

From the principles of Purity and Contentment, we move to a more deeply profound concept of self-mastery and soulful living—developing Discipline. The Sanskrit name for this principle is *Tapas*, which literally means "heat," as in "burning away" or removing whatever does not serve your well-being. It's important to burn away any impurities through strict self-discipline in three areas—the body, the mind, and speech.

For example, to discipline the body, you might go on a fast to cleanse your digestive system and organs, stay on a healthy food regimen, and exercise to burn calories. To discipline the mind, you might let go of memories of past hurts, stop thinking negative thoughts about things lacking in your life, and shift from judging to accepting people as they are.

Lastly, to discipline speech, you might be mindful not to say anything that might be offensive, tailor your speech to be consistently kind, and avoid engaging in gossip. Following this principle of *Tapas*, you develop the self-discipline to resist distractions, hone skills, and perform tasks required to excel in your career.

Can you recall resisting many distractions, like phone calls, favorite shows, and repeated snacking, to study for a high school or college exam or to complete a project with a deadline?

Practicing Discipline calls for developing austerity or rigorous performance that overcomes the pull of desires. It promotes endurance, willpower, and character building.

You develop the Discipline to burn away all impurities and eliminate desires that get in the way of achieving goals. In other words, with the goal in mind, just as one might do in yoga class, you *hold the pose through challenges* and reap the benefits.

Discipline with Compassion

"Effectiveness is, after all, not a 'subject,'

but a self-Discipline— rather than doing things right, doing the right things."

–Peter F. Drucker, American Business Consultant

While applying self-discipline, you must also practice Compassion, the primary principle. Discipline must never be brutal or hurtful but always tempered with loving kindness. Take, for example, an advertising executive who is spending the weekend working on a very important presentation for her company's biggest client on Monday. While she is driven to get it done and have it be excellent, she must also be kind to herself in the process. Although spending most of the day staring at the computer, she can refresh herself by taking breaks and perhaps go out in nature for a walk. She can stop to enjoy her favorite foods and make sure that she has enough sleep as she keeps working to complete her project.

During the weekend, her intense focus is on creating an excellent presentation, so she practices self-restraint to avoid activities that might distract her, such as long, chatty phone calls and favorite TV or internet pastimes. In this way, she is simultaneously practicing Discipline and Compassion for herself.

Discipline, or burning impurities, entails eliminating whatever might interfere with accomplishing the goal. Although Discipline suggests intense rigor, the message is an uplifting one. Being compassionate to yourself is having the Discipline to do what needs to be done. The idea is to develop greater zeal in keeping the promises you make to yourself for your own benefit and the welfare of others.

Tough Love, Will Power, and Being Fierce with Yourself

"One of the most crucial elements of determination is

daily discipline—doing what needs to be done

even when you don't feel like doing it."

– Connie Tang, Cisco Project Management Director

To summon the zeal of self-control, you need to access a place of inner strength, endurance, and willpower. Discipline can be viewed as tough love or being fierce with yourself to achieve what is beneficial. Being fierce with yourself means keeping your word to do what you say you will do. Sometimes it means pushing yourself when you don't feel like doing the work. Often being disciplined entails sticking with a project when it gets difficult. As this chapter's title states, being disciplined means you *hold the pose through challenges.*

Have you noticed that the promises people tend to break most easily are the ones we make to ourselves? Somehow, commitments made to others are the ones we find the strength to keep. How often have companions told us they were going to quit smoking, stop drinking, or diet to lose excess weight—but did not have the willpower to follow through?

I am reminded of Mark Twain's famous quotation about smoking. To paraphrase, he said, *"Giving up smoking is one of the easiest things in the world. I know because I've done it thousands of times."*

Be authentic and tell the truth to yourself if you are not ready to quit an indulgence, but think about how you might summon the willpower to do so in the future. Being fierce means saying, "That's it! I am quitting this now, or I am starting this now — no doubt about it—no ands, ifs, or buts! This ends now! That starts immediately!" Being fierce with yourself about the important things is like strong parenting. It entails emphatic resolve on your part to transcend any and all temptation to backslide—and to actually mean it this time. Being fierce with yourself can help you overcome the tendency to hold promises to yourself too lightly. And like a good parent, give yourself a reward for having the Discipline to achieve your goal.

It would be best if you were adamant, as in really meaning it, but never harsh. And if backsliding occurs, always remember to be compassionate to yourself. You might fall short once or twice before exerting your full willpower. Once you really commit to your well-being, the promises you make to nurture yourself will be the most important ones.

You become a crusader for your own well-being by practicing Discipline. I invite you to use this principle to reflect upon any current situations in your life that may require greater self-control or willpower and examine your efforts to achieve your most passionate goals.

Being Fierce with Myself—Doctoral Dissertation Writing Discipline

"Maturity is achieved when a person postpones immediate pleasures for long-term values."

– Joshua L. Liebman, American Rabbi and Author

A perfect example of being fierce with myself to summon Discipline relates to writing my long neglected doctoral dissertation. In 1992, when I left New York for a non-ending vacation in Sedona, Arizona, I had completed my doctoral coursework at New York University and was "ABD – All But Dissertation."

After camping out for over a year, I decided turn my passion for Yoga on the red rocks into a small business and gave birth to *Sedona Spirit Yoga & Hiking*, which has presently expanded to *Sedona Spirit Yoga, Healing, and Vortex Journeys*—now the winner of seven consecutive years of Best-of-Sedona Awards 2019-2025. When I left the NYC school system, creating this new tourist business was my full-time priority, and the idea of writing my Ph.D. dissertation was so far on the back burner that it was falling off the stove.

A few years later, I told myself that if I did not do something soon, my research would be outdated, and I would need to accept myself being only an "ABD" (All-But-Dissertation) and never a Ph.D. I could not let that happen! So, I summoned the Discipline to drive up to Northern Arizona University in Flagstaff and spent days in the library freshening up the research for my dissertation. Once my research was somewhat updated, there was still no attention to writing. My dissertation—ironically, on the topic of Writing Anxiety in Educational Professionals—was not happening.

Finally, I told myself, "Johanna, this is it! It's now or never. Just do it!" Being fierce with myself worked, and I came up with a plan. From my days in New York, I recalled a commercial announcing that "Wednesday is Prince Spaghetti Day!" (Funny, the things we remember!) Then, I decided to adopt that policy. Being compassionate to myself, I decided to focus on writing one day a week and declared that "Wednesday is Doctoral Dissertation Writing Day!"

So, I kept every Wednesday free and was riveted to my computer once I started. But it was so hard to get into the writing each Wednesday that I came up with the second part of my plan. To entice myself to the computer, I would allow myself to play Solitaire until I won and then get into writing for several hours. After many months of Wednesday Solitaire and dissertation writing, I spent more than a week at the computer finishing my masterpiece just in time for the flight to my dissertation review at New York University. I flew to New York and presented the dissertation to my dear Professor, John Mayher, and his committee colleagues. I was thrilled when they accepted it with a request for minor changes. Afterwards, they toasted my success with little plastic glasses of champagne. And I rewarded myself with a fun New York vacation with loving friends and family. It's always good to promise yourself a reward before you begin—a light shining at the end of your tunnel of Discipline.

So now I am Piled-High-and-Deep! I received my Ph.D. Diploma from New York University in May, 1995. My adamant self-discipline paid off. I encourage you to apply fierce but compassionate discipline with yourself for your important goals. And don't forget to set up a treat for yourself after your discipline brings success. It works!

Let's Refrain from Whipping Ourselves with "Shoulds and Shouldn'ts"

As part of human conditioning, people often tend to perpetuate the punishing aspect of Discipline mentioned earlier. When they go ahead and do something they lack the willpower to stop, they often apply the whip of self-criticism. For example, a man gives in to having a cigar when he says he wants to stop smoking. Instead of enjoying that cigar, he feels bad because he thinks he shouldn't be smoking. Or perhaps it's a dish of ice cream or a chocolate bar that is a woman's breach of self-restraint. Instead of savoring the sugary treats, she feels guilty before, during, and after the brief moment of indulgence.

Sometimes you can be self-disciplined, and other times you may backslide a bit. The important thing to remember is to be kind to yourself and enjoy whatever you decide to do. Consciously choosing Moderation is also a form of Discipline, and you can do so by practicing the paramount principle of Compassion for yourself.

Another instance of this punishing type of Discipline is when you may have something you must do but are not doing, and you chastise yourself with the idea that it needs to be done and you SHOULD be doing it. For example, I had a small black-and-white tile kitchen floor at a former home that showed every tiny spot. I would sometimes look at it as I left the house and say, "I really should wash that kitchen floor" and feel bad about it for a few moments. But if I had an important meeting that I didn't want to be late for, I would remember to be compassionate to myself and make a mental note to take care of it as soon as I could. In reality, it would take less than ten minutes to wash this little tile area. I am reminded of the Nike slogan, "Just do it!" Or, if you cannot do it now, let it go, and don't feel bad about not doing it.

In contrast to the punishing aspect of Discipline, there are the very many rewards that accrue from being disciplined so that you can achieve good things like a vibrant, healthy body, a clean environment, professional diplomas and other credentials, and success in all your endeavors. After being fierce with yourself to get the challenging job done, don't forget to give yourself a reward for your disciplined perseverance.

There's a colloquial expression, "When you're hot, you're hot, and when you're not, you're not!" Well, the same goes for this principle — "When you are disciplined, you're disciplined, and when you're not, you're not." Let us all beware of not beating ourselves up with "shoulds and shouldn'ts" and allow ourselves to be human while holding high standards for our behavior. Remember the two important principles that accompany Discipline, and be sure to practice both Compassion and Moderation.

Benefits of Practicing Discipline

"Tapas is derived from the root 'tap' meaning to blaze, burn, shine, suffer pain or consume by heat. It… means a burning effort under all circumstances to achieve a definite goal in life. The whole science of character building may be regarded as a practice of tapas."

– B.K.S. Iyengar, Indian Yoga Master

Mastering *Tapas* or Discipline brings about many rewards. As B.K.S. Iyengar notes above, practicing Discipline builds character. ***The Yoga Sutras*** claim that having the Discipline to purge impurities helps you refine your inner being and access your full potential and greatest power. Discipline helps you strive to be the best person you can be. It guides you to bypass the many distracting facets of life that pull you away from achieving your goals for success. Discipline fosters integrity and helps you get in touch with the deepest part of yourself.

Tapas helps you through the uncomfortable sensations in Yoga postures on the mat or in roles you play in life. It motivates you to try more challenging maneuvers and reach higher. Discipline helps you develop your inner strength and willpower and empowers your performance in everyday life.

Everyday Examples of Lack of Discipline

The following are examples of the need for self-discipline in mind, body, and speech. See if you can relate to any of them--

- Going off your diet or exercise plan
- Being too tired to take care of personal well-being
- Blurting out a tirade against someone
- Failing to keep commitments to self and others
- Allowing distractions to interfere with performance
- Attending a meeting without being fully prepared
- Accidentally saying insensitive things
- Not being able to focus your mind on the goal
- Operating at 75% of your usual capacity
- Leaning on others to do your job

Discussion and Journal Writing on Discipline--Good Notices, Ahas, Gratitude, Fun Scribbling, Shifts, Intentions, Self-Care

- What comes to mind when you reflect on Discipline?
- In what areas of your life are you most disciplined in your endeavors?
- In what circumstances do you find yourself lacking discipline?
- Is there a current situation in which you might need to apply greater discipline to achieve a goal?
- Can you recall a past goal that you pursued with great fervor or tapas, and the results you accomplished?

Ways to Practice Discipline

To develop greater Discipline, I will be rigorous in my commitment to take the following steps:

- I will practice greater Discipline, doing what's best to nurture my body with daily exercise, the right foods, and restful sleep.
- I will Discipline my mind and speech to release negative words and refrain from judging other people or gossiping about anyone.
- I will summon the Discipline to apply undistracted effort to complete actions and projects on my longtime, neglected to-do list.

If you now see any ways you might apply greater rigor to achieve important goals, you are successfully engaging in Discipline.

Affirmations

- I am in control of my bodily desires
- I am mindful of my speech
- I am watchful over my thoughts
- I have a burning desire to achieve my goals
- I am disciplined in my spiritual endeavors
- I passionately overcome obstacles to the highest good

"Drop In" for Discipline

- Sit in a quiet place and close your eyes
- Breathe into feeling the love in your heart
- Label exterior sensations and let them go
- Nestle into a peaceful, loving place within
- Appreciate yourself for having the discipline to excel at your goals
- Thank the Universe for the goodness of life

Svadhyaya

Thirsting for purpose
Learning, reflecting on self
The chalice receives

CHAPTER NINE

◇ ◇ ◇

Self-Study—
Reflect on Your Practice

The Fourth *Niyama:* The Yoga Principle
SVADHYAYA, Self-Study

How often do you reflect on what's working best and what needs to shift in your daily life?

"When you stop learning, you stop growing."

—Ken Blanchard, American Business Consultant

The fourth personal growth principle for soulful living is called *Svadhyaya* in Sanskrit, *Sva* meaning "self" and *adhyaya* meaning "the study of." This practice advocates ongoing reflection and Self-Study to maximize your strengths. Whenever you make self-assessments, always inquire without allowing any blame or harsh judgment. *Reflect on your practice* and be grateful for whatever you notice. And remember my earlier advice to congratulate yourself on whatever you may discover and say "Good Notice!"

Take a few moments to ask yourself—What are my strengths?"Then take time to reflect upon— What weaknesses might I improve?" You could even draw a line down the center of a piece of paper, and list your strengths on one side and your shortcomings on the other.

The Wisdom of Self-Study

"This is your one and only precious life.

Somebody's going to decide how it's going to be lived,

and that person had better be you."

– Stan Slap, American Business Author

It's really not about labeling yourself as "weak" or "strong" in different areas. It's more about reflecting on how you can heighten your most positive qualities, refine any less-than-glowing aspects of your being, and develop your higher consciousness.

This principle teaches you to cultivate your best self and discover your life purpose. In ancient times, *Svadhyaya* alluded to reading sacred scriptures and gathering in *satsangas*, or "meetings in truth," intended to raise consciousness. Today, it can be broadened to include expanding self-awareness and learning from others through uplifting gatherings, worthwhile reading, internet viewing, and spiritual practice. These actions will help lead you to communion with your core goodness and Universal Oneness.

While applying this principle of ongoing Self Study, you can learn to practice constant awareness that is free of blame.

You can become the non-judgmental, discerning witness of your actions. As you learn to reflect upon your moment-to-moment behavior, you can use the ten principles in this book as your standards and return to them whenever you veer off course.

As you develop greater awareness, you can learn to monitor your thoughts, actions, and speech daily. Rather than have a fixed worldview, you can remain open to reflection and change.

While performing your various day-to-day roles, you can take time to review how well you are connecting with other people. You can *reflect on your practice* to keep your heart open and engaged in life experiences to heighten your consciousness and contribute to others.

How Are You Filling Your Sacred Chalice?

"We do not learn from experience....

we learn from reflecting on experience."

—John Dewey, American Philosopher

For this principle of Self-Study, I like to use the metaphor of each person being a sacred chalice—a gorgeous, golden, jeweled goblet like those belonging to medieval knights.

The concept is similar to the emotional bucket-filling mentioned earlier in the chapter on being heart-centered, but more beautiful and elegant to represent your sacred self and soulful living.

Perhaps you can think of yourself as an empty chalice to be filled with whatever you choose to put inside. Moment-to-moment, as you *reflect on your practice,* you can be aware of what you are taking into your heart, mind, and body.

As you monitor your intake of life experiences, you can choose activities to enhance your aliveness and learn to recognize and release those that may be less beneficial, perhaps even harmful or toxic. Take a moment to think about what you are filling your chalice with these days.

Pursuing Activities That Help You Grow

"Your perspective is always limited by how much you know. Expand your knowledge and you will transform your mind."

—Bruce H. Lipton, Developmental Biologist

Pursuing the highest, clearest, and brightest energy you can find, aim to engage in meaningful events or entertainment with others and in worthwhile reading or internet viewing. You can take time to read works by master thinkers and experts on a variety of topics, either in print or online.

The principle of Self-Study encourages joining group activities so that you can learn from being with people who are focused on personal growth. You can choose to attend whatever church, synagogue, or spiritual service you are called to, but participation does not have to be religious in nature.

Too often, people may allow their monkey mind's random thought process to keep them feeling separate much of the time. It is important to get out of the habit of keeping yourself separate and perhaps somewhat isolated.

You can participate in environmental agencies that care for our earth, such as Habitat for Humanity or the Humane Society. You can join any group encouraging positive values and healthy participation. Examples are your company's athletic team, your local Chamber of Commerce, or senior citizens' group. You might attend enriching events at your community center or neighborhood bookstore. You can expand your knowledge in your field of interest by joining professional groups and attending their events. Volunteering to work at the library, participating in a writing group, or attending a Yoga or meditation class are all beneficial ways of engaging in positive interaction with others. You can enjoy spiritual and religious gatherings of your choice that you find uplifting. The idea is to participate in new experiences that can promote your personal growth and make you feel good about yourself, others, and life in general.

"Before you can move in new directions,

you must first let go of what's not working for you."

—Alberto Villoldo, Psychologist, Shaman and Author

Studying yourself entails taking time to go inward more often, *reflect on your practice*, and develop the ability to access and clear your inner feelings.

You can slow down, become more aware, and reflect on how you treat yourself and others. You can make it a regular practice to pause often to look at how you are living your life.

Expanding Consciousness Through Prayer

"More things are wrought by prayer than this world dreams of.

—Lord Alfred Tennyson

Ultimately, true Self-Study entails going deeper within to discover and feel your connectedness with all that is, your Oneness with the Divine Energy of which we are all made. This principle invites you to still the automatic monkey mind and find the sacred peace we all have within. It calls for you to focus on a Higher Power and deepen your devotion through prayer, mantra, or whatever way is comfortable for you.

There are many forms of prayer that can help you connect with your sense of the Divine Power in the Universe. You can say traditional prayers from your religious upbringing or develop your own way of conversing with the Divine Intelligence or All-Being, Universal Consciousness.

I have found it strengthening to shift from prayer that pleads for help to prayer that expresses gratitude for assistance that is already on the way. Instead of saying, "Please help me with this...," I might say, "Thank you, God, for guiding me through this challenge. I feel your Presence." That way, I immediately have the comfort of Divine support upon uttering the prayer.

The idea is to avoid pleading prayers that focus on the lack of what you are praying for. For example, if you are praying for greater prosperity, an affirmative prayer would be to thank God for helping you earn more money to cover expenses, and a pleading prayer would be lamenting the shortage of funds and asking for strength to deal with not being able to pay all of the bills this month. Pleading prayers that focus on what's missing echo and reinforce that scarcity. It is commonly acknowledged in quantum physics and the law of attraction that thoughts, like atoms, are drawn towards the same kind of thoughts.

So, we get what we believe and what we give attention to in our consciousness. Do you want to have your prayers spotlight what you don't want or what you do want? Affirmative prayers, expressing trust that you are receiving Divine blessings, focus on your belief in the abundant goodness of the Universe and place your attention on having what you desire.

Whenever I am praying for something specific, I always ask God to provide it only "if it is in the highest good for all concerned." If my prayer is not answered, I then assume it might not now be for the greatest good.

How you pray and to whom you pray is for you to decide. Whatever your choices might be, the act of engaging in prayer helps you connect with a benevolent Higher Power and surrender to the Invisible Universe beyond your control. Prayer widens your personal perspective and expands your consciousness from a myopic focus on your own little life story to the big picture, where unseen forces are at play in the Universe.

Raising Consciousness with Mantras

In addition to various forms of prayer, there is the practice of repeating a short phrase or mantra to connect with Spirit and raise consciousness. In all languages, the single syllable "Om" or "Aum" is the Universal sound of peace or the name of God. There are innumerable Sanskrit mantras and chants that call upon the various forms of God and the Divine Mother, and every tradition has its own holy words and phrases

The repetition of a mantra is beneficial in any language. It is a way of connecting with Spirit or Divine Source and a way of calling for goodness in life. A simple, yet powerful, way to use mantra repetition is to create your own mantras in English, such as "Be still and know that all is well." Mantras do not necessarily have to refer to deities but can allude to whatever you choose to manifest in your life.

Actually, a mantra can be any affirmation or positive thought that you choose to repeat over and over again to strengthen yourself and uplift your consciousness. Examples are: "My peace is more important than this; I am filled with love and light; I let go and trust life."

Just as it is important to stay conscious of each word while uttering prayers in any religion, such as on rosary beads in Catholicism, repeating each mantra with feeling is essential. As you know, affirmations do not work unless they are felt within your energy field, and it is the same with mantras. Whatever form of prayer or mantra you may choose, it is vital for you to have your own way of connecting with a Higher Power and tapping into your spirituality as often as possible.

Find Peace and Purpose Through Reflection

"Your beliefs become your thoughts. Your thoughts become your words. Your words become your actions. Your actions become your habits. Your habits become your values. Your values become your destiny."

– Mahatma Gandhi, Leader of Non-Violence

As you learn to reflect on your experiences using these ten Yoga principles as your guidelines, you can learn to accept all life's experiences with grace and cultivate a deeper sense of peace within. Then you can bring this lighthearted, good-natured attitude to everything you do, removing obstacles and expressing yourself with kindness and sensitivity. When you are at peace, you are more centered and receptive to life's messages.

When you frequently *reflect on your practice*, you can better recognize the aspects of your life that are rewarding and those that are not. Peaceful reflection, without judgment or blame, helps you discern the value of what you just did and inquire into what might be beneficial to do next. Ongoing Self-Study is like a great GPS that shows you a map of networks you have already traveled and those you can pursue to increase well-being for yourself and others. As poet Robert Frost would say, reflection helps you become aware of "The Road Not Taken." It opens you up to a wide array of possible steps you can take to enrich yourself and contribute to others.

Personally, I have had numerous rewarding career shifts prompted by ongoing reflection. After being a high school English teacher for over twenty-five years, I became interested in Yoga and shifted my purpose to contribute to the peaceful well-being of my students rather than their literacy education. Through years of Yoga and meditation practice, teaching, and study, my deepening self-reflection brought me to a higher spiritual perspective.

As mentioned earlier, my Self-Study called me to go on a sabbatical from teaching English in New York City public high schools to visit Sedona, Arizona, where I camped out for over a year, fourteen months to be exact. On this vacation, my reflection led me to first retire from teaching in New York City and then make a new career out of leading Sedona Spirit Yoga and Hiking vortex journeys and retreats.

Upon being introduced to Richard Miller's iRest Inner Restoration Yoga Nidra in 2013, I was inspired to pursue my certification as a Level III Master Practitioner of Yoga Nidra Meditation within the next three to four years. Since then, I have been offering Yoga Nidra sessions as a way to help myself and my clients access inner being and clear thoughts and emotions held deep within. Yoga Nidra has proven successful in helping troubled veterans of war zones and women rescued from human trafficking. I found it to be a very effective, deeply rewarding way to help clients release past traumas.

Later, in 2018, at a vacation retreat with Alberto Villoldo in Peru, I was deeply moved to pursue intensive training in Shamanic Energy Medicine (from 2019-2021) as a way to clear the body's pent-up energy and promote healing to restore ultimate well-being. Finally, practicing this Shamanic energy medicine enabled me to help people heal deep emotional wounds. In this hands-on 300-hour program, I received training in numerous Shamanic medicine practices to test clients' chakras, help them clear out blocks, and see their energy transform right before my eyes.

As a life-long learner, I continue to embrace new ideas and ways of thinking, being, and healing. I found Yoga Nidra to be an enlightening expansion of the healing depths of Yoga. When I was introduced to Peruvian Shamanism, I was uplifted by a deeper connection to the healing nature of Mother Earth, the animal kingdom, human consciousness, and the celestial forces of the Universe. Recently, my self-reflection led me to pursue advanced PSYCH-K® Facilitator courses to learn processes to help me shift my unconscious limiting beliefs and those of my clients. And, there is so much more to learn as I continue to expand my consciousness and contribute to others.

I would never have been able to grow into these new career roles had I not taken the time to reflect on what I was currently doing and what was calling me forth. That's my *Dharma*, a Sanskrit word for "purpose" or "right calling." And I have had a passion for writing since high school, so writing books is also my *Dharma.* We all know people who are shifting careers as they reflect upon how they want to use their energy to help others. How about YOU?

What is Your Dharma?

"Learn to transform body, mind, and spirit as a prelude to transforming self, culture, and world."

– Ken Wilbur, American Writer and Public Speaker

Part of Self-Study is asking what contributions you want to make, finding out what services you are here to give to others, and getting clear on your purpose for living. "What have you been doing?" and "What would you like to do next?" are ongoing questions that offer the freedom of choice to motivate taking action when steps become clear.

I recommend patience to those of you who are aware that your current career is not fulfilling your *Dharma* or right calling. My shifts occurred gradually over decades of maturity and study. It is fine to take time to inquire about what might be most fulfilling for you and to plant seeds to manifest that when the time is right. This type of moment-to-moment engagement and reflective Self-Study can help you be the best you can be. It can also help you become clear on how you can contribute more to others and fulfill your purpose for living.

Look in the Mirror and Ask, "How am I Doing?"

"You are the master of your destiny. You can influence, direct, and control your own environment. You can make your life what you want it to be."

– Napoleon Hill, American Self-Help Author

As self-reflective, developing beings, it is helpful to frequently ask ourselves, "How am I doing?" This used to be a favorite expression of New York City's Mayor Koch decades ago.

The Earth School's classes and corridors are filled with mirrors. Each interaction and event reflects something back to you about yourself. It is your job to become increasingly aware of life's messages and more open to receiving them when you *reflect on your practice.*

For example, if someone becomes annoyed at something you have said or done, it is best not to dismiss them. You might mentally inquire into what may have offended them. Of course, you probably think that what you said or did was fine, but perhaps you could have presented yourself in a way that would have been better received. Maybe there was negative energy you projected without realizing it.

And, maybe their response had nothing to do with you. You can be confident enough to reflect on ways you might have improved your interactions without taking anything personally. There are those moments when everyone wishes they could simply review what just happened and be granted a "do-over." Without magnifying anything from its proper perspective, it is good to learn from what you see being reflected. Just observe your effect on the people around you. When something seems unharmonious, simply recognize it. Say, "Good notice!" and see if you can shift things for the better.

There is a common metaphor that the people you come across in life serve as "mirrors," in which you see a reflection of yourself. In the spirit of personal growth, you can remain open to viewing what the mirrors are reflecting back.

When you see others who are unhappy with you, be open to look at their point of view, address where there might be validity in their perceptions, and perhaps shift your attitude or behavior. Yes, you can learn a lot from what the mirrors reflect; they often reveal your blind spots and unconscious projections.

Moments of Self-Reflection and Shift

"Everything you experience mirrors a part of you."

—Alberto Villoldo, Psychologist, Shaman and Author

I recall being in a store with a long check-out line that did not seem to move. I was late for an appointment, and my automatic mind started to mentally berate the girl at the register, thinking she must be the slowest check-out person on the planet. My mind rattled on as I wondered if she was stoned or something.

Then, as I listened to myself complain, I realized I was being unkind and decided to be patient and friendly. As the tired clerk totaled my merchandise, I softly asked, "Has it been a very busy day?" She replied that she was working extra hours because another employee had called in sick. I was really glad that I had made the quick shift before I got to the front of this overworked cashier's line.

Another example is when I was leading a wonderful and happy retreat group, and a couple of guests in the back of my van were talking so loudly that I could not point out places of interest. I turned around and asked if I could have a moment to share what we were about to do. Suddenly, there was dead silence and then a long, awkward pause.

Feeling the energy of the two ladies behind me plummet, I turned to the one I could see and asked if I had offended her. She immediately told me that her mother had always yelled at her to "shh" and be quiet. My comment had prompted fear and a host of sad, hurt feelings. Once she acknowledged the association with her mother that carried over to me, she was able to let it go and participated joyfully again with me and the group.

Sometimes the feelings you evoke in others go deeper than what is happening in that moment. They may not have anything to do with you personally. The point is that when you are attuned to the energy flow of harmony, you can feel when something is out of sync and clear it up. That is one of the greatest benefits of Self-Study.

By *reflecting on your practice*, you can explore every facet of being human and anything that will help you understand yourself better. You can learn to recognize what frequently presses your buttons and spot the potholes you tend to fall into most often. As you grow in awareness, you can learn to use your strengths to overcome your less-developed features, aka "weaknesses." Through such Self-Study, you nurture the core essence within and enhance the Oneness you share with all others. You expand your consciousness to include the viewpoints of others and see the big picture beyond your myopic self-interest.

Benefits of Practicing Self-Study

"The more effective our study, the more we understand our weaknesses and strengths. We learn to minimize our weaknesses and maximize our strengths. Then, there is no limit to our understanding."

– T.K.V. Desikachar, Indian Yoga Master

Ongoing Self-Study offers tremendous rewards. The sages teach that practicing frequent self-reflection brings us closer and closer to knowing the Conscious Intelligence Field of all that is. If all beings are one, the better you know yourself, the better you can understand others and connect with the Divine Source of the Universe that bonds everyone.

Through enriching reading, activities, heart-felt prayer, and mantra, you can become clearer in each moment about who you are and what you have to contribute. Instead of being static or set in your ways, you can be open to raising yourself to higher and higher states of being. With ongoing Self-Study, you can become a lifelong learner, always expanding in consciousness, discovering and pursuing your life's purpose.

As you practice Self-Study, life becomes enhanced. You meet more interesting people, read great books, view uplifting programs that change your thinking, and attend gatherings that broaden your perspectives. Your life becomes an adventure in personal growth and achievement. You are always passionately growing and raising your consciousness to a higher plane. For developing beings, engaging in Self-Study is your life-long quest to keep learning, growing, and contributing the best you have to offer.

Examples of the Need to Practice Self-Study

Review the following examples of the need for greater Self-Study and discernment. See if any of them might be similar to what you experience--

- Not taking time to reflect on how you are living your life
- Being too busy to notice how your actions affect others
- Plodding on from day to day without really knowing your purpose
- Being too closed to shift to a new perspective
- Feeling obligated to spend time with people who are often negative
- Postponing uplifting gatherings that you keep hoping to attend
- Knowing what would be good for you but not doing it
- Getting adamant and fixed in your opinions of people and things
- Watching shows and reading literature with harmful, decadent content
- Never taking time to still yourself and access inner guidance

Discussion and Journal Writing on Self-Study-- Good Notices, Ahas, Gratitude, Fun Scribbling, Shifts, Intentions, Self-Care

- What does the principle of Self-Study suggest to you?
- What do you do to engage in reflection and self-study?
- How might reflecting on your life experience help you achieve greater fulfillment?
- What is the last spiritual experience you had, and what did it teach you about yourself?
- How would you answer the following questions? – "Who am I?" "What is my purpose in life?"
- What additional activities can you pursue to engage in enlightening self-study?

Ways to Practice Greater Self-Study

To cultivate my best self, I will take the following measures to practice Self-Study:

- I will be mindful to choose companions, activities, and entertainment that are consciousness-raising for my highest good.
- I will take time each day to reflect on my performance at work and home, asking myself, "How am I doing?" to make sure that I am doing my best.
- I will raise my consciousness beyond my personal needs and desires by spending time in prayer and service for the well-being of others.

As you take time to reflect upon your daily life, you have started a very beneficial lifelong practice of Self-Study.

Affirmations

- I am a lifelong learner
- I study to develop my higher self
- I gather in truth with other spiritual beings
- I uplift my soul in prayer and mantra
- I live a life of reflection
- I embrace my connection to Source

"Drop In" for Self-Study

- Sit in a quiet place and close your eyes
- Breathe into feeling the love in your heart
- Label exterior sensations and let them go
- Nestle into a peaceful, loving place within
- Appreciate yourself for being reflective and open to change
- Thank the Universe for the goodness of life

Ishvara-Pranidhana

Surpassing ego
Surrendering to Divine Light
The rainbow rejoices

CHAPTER TEN

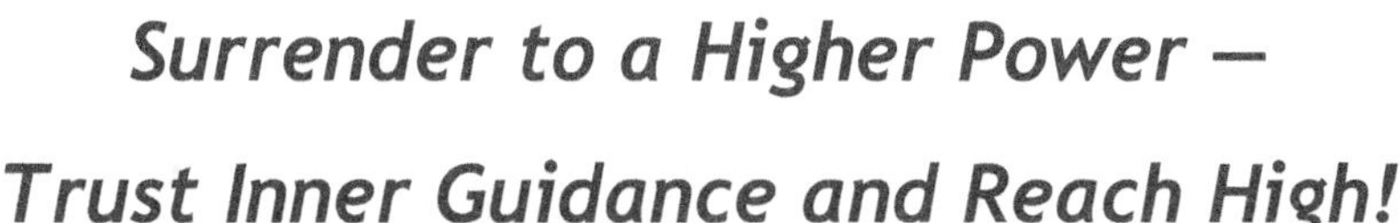

Surrender to a Higher Power – Trust Inner Guidance and Reach High!

The Fifth *Niyama:* The Yoga Principle
ISHVARA PRANIDHANA,
Surrender to a Higher Power

Can you trust that although you are not in control, the Universe somehow always takes care of you?

You may have seen the brightly colored nests of Russian dolls that fit inside each other. Imagine that you are like a Russian nest of dolls, and we have just gone through all your layers of being (your different-sized dolls from the large outer you to the medium and small layers of your more internal being).

Following the last four principles of Purity, Contentment, Discipline, and Self-Study prepares you to access the deepest and purest part of yourself and *reach high* into your Universal Consciousness.

Once you purify your life to achieve greater clarity, assert discipline to pursue higher goals, and reflect on ways to constantly upgrade your performance, you are ready to look at your deepest nature.

We have now arrived at your littlest doll, which glows at your center, representing your innermost being. This core part of your being is your essence, your place of inner knowing, your spiritual nature, your moral goodness guide, and your source of connectedness to all of life.

This is the Highest Consciousness you can rise into. Your inner Light Being is the wise witness of everything that happens to you, the sage seer that evaluates options, reflects on your performance, and makes ongoing decisions. It is your soul's connection to the entire Universe and every creature in it.

Surrender to Your Highest Power

The zenith of our ten ancient principles is the call to surrender to a Higher Power. The Sanskrit name *Ishvara Pranidhana* literally translates as *Ishvara*, defined as "God," and *Pranidhana*, meaning "surrender." Surrender in this context means learning to trust the Higher Power that exists within you and throughout everything in the entire Universe. It dedicates your actions and will to the Supreme Beingness we all share—the Divine Source inherent in all life and the highest good. It is devotion to the Inner Light or pulse shared by every being.

By practicing surrender, when things you do not like happen, you trust that somehow everything is as it was meant to be. When faced with things you do not know how to accomplish or do not understand how to solve, you do your best and surrender them to Higher Consciousness, asking for guidance. This is not surrendering in the sense of loss but in the sense of letting go of your ego's desire to control outcomes from a mental place, replacing it with heart-centered faith and trust in the creative Consciousness of the Universe. In surrendering, you do not lose any part of yourself or take anything from anyone else. You are simply ceding control to the Invisible Power or Cosmic Energy orchestrating events behind the scenes.

> *"Ishvara Pranidhana is a life of dedication, of offering everything to the Lord or to humanity. Why do I add humanity? When we want to offer something to God, where and who is He/She/It? Is God sitting somewhere waiting for us to give Him something? God made the world.... The world itself is God. All that is outside us is God. When we dedicate ourselves to the benefit of humanity, we have dedicated ourselves to God."*
>
> –Swami Satchidananda, Indian Yoga Master

Surrender Your Ego's Myopic View and Focus on the Big Picture

What is your ego, and how is it both your friend and your enemy? The ego is "a person's sense of self-esteem, self-importance, self-respect, self-image, or self-confidence. It is part of the mind that usually mediates between the conscious and unconscious and is responsible for reality testing and a sense of personal identity." [40]

Maintaining a healthy ego is very important to succeed in life. Yet, when your ego is inflated, life becomes all about you and your personal perspective, with a narrow focus on "I, Me, My" and fulfilling your needs and desires. Yes, it is important to take care of your needs and, at the same time, see yourself as part of a larger Universe that calls for you to keep expanding your perspective and your contributions to others. With a healthy ego, you see yourself playing a small part in the big picture of life. You realize that there is an Intelligence larger than yourself, guiding and directing the course of events.

Letting go of ego means being present to what is rather than what you want. It entails keeping an eye on how you are interrelated with everything and everyone and recognizing that an Omnipresent Force in the Universe orchestrates what happens. Surrendering myopic concern with promoting your own welfare can be truly freeing, for you can be happiest if you align with whatever may happen (practicing the principle of Contentment) and feel that the will of the Universe is your will.

You can perform actions as a contribution to the well-being of others. Happy to be of service, you can let go of any illusion of control. You can learn to stop fostering separation and highlighting differences between you and your fellow human beings. When you surrender to the Spirit of your Highest Being within, you connect with a sense of Oneness and community instead of separation and competition. As you *trust your inner guidance and reach high* into your soul essence, there is no longer any separation, just Oneness with the All-Being Life Impulse everyone shares.

---

[40] http://www.differencebetween.net

To live in service to the highest good for all mankind is the ultimate surrender of your ego's passionate striving to control outcomes. Life is not about fulfilling your ego's desires but about something much bigger—the harmony of the whole Universe.

This does not suggest that you deprive yourself, but that you put personal needs in proper perspective within a larger context. There is a flow to how things happen in life. You can either surrender to that flow or resist and get caught up in your disappointment.

At times, you may even overdramatize challenging experiences into misery. Suffering stems from not accepting what is. Once you surrender and accept what happens, you can restore harmony to your being, relationships, and surroundings.

While you do not have control, you do have input. Following this principle of surrender, you are encouraged to develop trust that whatever happens is, somehow, for the highest good. Everyone has had the experience of watching a plan fail and having something better happen in its place. The best advice is to make plans, take steps to have them succeed, and let go of any attachment to the outcome.

Surrendering Is Strength, Not Defeat

"You will be amazed at how things fall magically into place once you let go of the illusion of control."[41]

The fifth and ultimate soulful living principle, *Ishvara Pranidhana,* calls for you to *trust your inner guidance and reach high.* It teaches you to surrender your ego to this Higher Power that is within you and throughout all of existence, however you might relate to it. The most common connotation

[41] http://www.bestofeveryquote.blogspot.com

of the word "surrender" is to concede defeat, as in waving a white flag on a battlefield.

No one wants to surrender and admit defeat in an argument, sporting game, or battle. Such surrender seems negative and like an admission of weakness or loss. In contrast, there is a very positive form of surrender, which is having the strength of faith to give up trying to control how things turn out. For example, we all have planned to take trips and have had the Universe make it easy to get time off from work and find affordable flights and hotels. At other times, we may want to go somewhere, and the Universe seems to keep blocking the path of travel with unavailability.

Once, I was trying to get award flights to and from Hawaii for a writing conference and was told that they were unavailable each time I searched online for a matter of weeks, no matter how I adjusted the dates.

Then it came to me that I was "pushing the river," and perhaps this conference that I was intent on attending was not right for me at this time. Sometimes when your path is blocked, it is because you are being guided in another direction.

You simply plant seeds, create intentions, do your best job, and surrender any attempts to sway circumstances. Yes, you do have input, but the truth is that you have no power beyond that. The only thing you have authority over is your own mind's reaction to whatever life brings.

Life's outcomes are not in your hands, so you might as well give up the illusion of control. What there is to surrender is your ego's attachment to having things work out your way.

Let's take a look at your beliefs about any "Invisible Powers" that may be orchestrating events behind the scenes of your life.

What Do You Believe In?

"The most important thing is not to stop questioning. Curiosity has its own reason for existing. One cannot help but be in awe when he contemplates the mysteries of eternity, of life, of the marvelous structure of reality. It is enough if one tries merely to comprehend a little of this mystery every day. Never lose a holy curiosity."

—Albert Einstein, Physicist and Nobel Laureate

We translate Ishvara Pranidhana as surrender to a "Higher Power," knowing that the term "God" ruffles some feathers. The question of belief in God is a delicate one. There are myriad definitions of what individuals may call God. You are to be respected for your beliefs and disbeliefs, no matter what they are. Some of you may have a strong belief in God. Others may question the existence of God. With deep respect for every religious credo and culture, all beliefs and religious practices are welcome.

Nevertheless, you cannot deny that there are forces present in the Universe that are more powerful than mankind, forces that transcend religious separation, uniting all in one vast Quantum Energy Field.

There are some things that are beyond our comprehension and control. We can call this Powerful Energy many things: the Prime Mover, the Great Spirit, the Divine Intelligence, the Omnipresent Force, the Eternal Consciousness, the Cosmic Vibration, the Supreme Goodness, the Creative Source, the Universal Flow, the Great Mystery, Nature, Mother Earth, or even God – whatever works for you.

"God is a feeling…a feeling of bliss. As we let go of everything in our lives that is not bliss, we experience God, our true nature, more fully."

–Michael Mirdad, Spiritual Teacher and Author

The Yoga teachings speak of God "as the perfect being pervading all things, the life of the world, the inner impulse of which each one of us has a share."[42] This "inner impulse" that connects and sustains each of us is what I call the "Soul." Honoring whatever religious or atheistic beliefs people may have about God, you cannot deny that there is this "inner impulse" everyone shares. This connectedness is ever-present, no matter how separate anyone may feel at times. You can expand your perceptions to *reach high* and recognize the all-pervading goodness (God-ness) that permeates existence and the natural flow of life that is beyond human control.

Religions as Paths to the Highest Goodness within You and the Universe

"The inspiration you seek is already within you.

Be silent and listen."

—Rumi, Thirteenth Century Persian Poet

One of my long-time best friends, Pesi, the wife of the late Rabbi Yankel Dinnerstein, devoutly observes the holy day of Shabbat, withdrawing from the material world into prayer every Friday night and Saturday. I admire her for this sacred commitment to go inside and experience her deepest connection with the highest Divine Energy running through her and all of the Universe.

I have come to understand that whatever religious practices you may pursue, those are the right ones to help you connect your inner being with the vast Conscious Intelligence Field. I see religions as pathways for all

[42] Wood, Ernest, *Great Systems of Yoga* (Maryland: Penguin Books, 1962), p. 26.

souls to connect with our deeper selves and the Highest Good of humanity. I was a devout Catholic until I married a Jewish man and could no longer go to the altar to receive communion, though not officially excommunicated. This made me feel not welcome or worthy, so I left the church to pursue a more general spiritual path. However, if I am ever afraid, I find great comfort in repeating the Hail Mary prayer.

I would never resonate with those who call themselves "recovering Catholics" because I am a "treasuring Catholic." While I no longer practice Catholicism, it still lives within me. I cherish the way the nuns at Holy Rosary Elementary School taught me to feel the Divine Presence of God and pray from a sacred place deep within.

So, whether you are an atheist, a devout believer, a Christian, a Jew, a member of any other religion, a nature lover, or just someone who describes yourself as "spiritual," it is all good as long as it connects you with your best self and a feeling of Oneness with all of existence.

Following this tenth principle, you surrender to the Spirit of your Highest Being within, and you *trust your inner guidance.* In doing so, you can embrace Divine Love and reverence for all life.

About the Conscious Intelligence Field

"The visible and invisible worlds are inextricably intertwined....
Once you've opened your eyes to this,
you can dance between them."

—Alberto Villoldo, Psychologist, Shaman, Author

In his book, *The Spontaneous Fulfillment of Desire*, Deepak Chopra delineates dual aspects of being, noting that we have both local and non-local aspects of our soul. These local and nonlocal energy sources affect our choices at any given time. Both are forces of goodness we connect with to varying degrees as we tap our inner knowing and create a clearer connection to the Universal Energies that guide us with messages.

Using an ocean metaphor, Deepak Chopra notes that our local existence is like being waves that are a small part of the vastness of the non-local ocean that is the essence of everything in the physical world. Chopra further describes the interrelationship of the local and non-local dimensions of our soul, noting that--

"Once we define the soul as deriving from the non-local, or virtual, realm, then our place in the universe becomes remarkably clear: We are both local and non-local, an individual pattern emerging from non-local intelligence, which is also part of everyone and everything else. We can think of the soul then as having two parts. The vast, non-local soul exists at the virtual or spirit level. It is powerful, pure, and capable of anything. The personal, local part of the soul exists at the quantum level. This is what reaches into our daily lives and holds the essence of who we are. It, too, is powerful, pure, and capable of anything. The same unbounded potential of the Infinite Spirit also resides in each and every one of us. Our personal soul, which we think of when we think of our 'selves,' is an outcropping of the eternal soul. If we could learn to live from the level of the soul, we would see that the best, most luminous part of ourselves is connected to the

rhythms of the Universe. We would truly know ourselves as the miracle-makers we are capable of being." [43]

Alberto Villoldo echoes this ocean metaphor, noting that--"We are like a drop of water in a vast, divine ocean, distinct yet immersed in something much larger than ourselves. It's only when we experience our connection to infinity that we're able to dream powerfully." [44]

This gives us quite a bit to ponder. You may choose to re-read these quotations and take a little time to digest them, as I did. Thinking of ourselves as waves in the ocean is definitely an image that shows us to be individual entities, connected to each other and held together by a vast ocean of Cosmic Energy.

The Magic of Soul Connection and Prayer

"One of the first ways that we can practice Ishvara Pranidhana is by putting aside some time each day, even a few minutes, to avail ourselves of an intelligence larger than our own.... This practice requires that we have recognized that there is some omnipresent force larger than ourselves that is guiding and directing the course of our lives."

—Donna Farhi, American Yoga Master

While in the process of drafting this chapter, I awoke one night at about four am with thoughts about surrendering to God running through my head, as if being downloaded to me from somewhere above. I immediately went into my home office, found a notepad, and started scribbling. The idea came that the purpose of surrendering the ego is to

[43] Chopra, Deepak, *The Essential Spontaneous Fulfillment of Desire: The Essence of Harnessing the Infinite Power of Coincidence* (New York: Harmony Books, 2003), p. 76.

[44] http://www.thefourwinds.com

establish a deeper "Connection" to your own spiritual self and all other spirits in the world. This union with your sacred self and others is beyond your ego, personality, roles, responsibilities, habits, likes, and dislikes. It is your inner knowing, your capacity to connect, your witness consciousness, and your ability to receive from the wonders of existence.

What there is to surrender is your ego's narrow focus on your personal pursuits and drama by letting go of having life be all about you, so you can experience the larger picture and consider the roles, relationships, and well-being of others for everyone's highest good. This surrendering of the ego launches you into a greater opening to receive the bounty that the Universe has in store for you.

And, we can leave the notion of "surrender" out of the picture altogether and adopt the interpretation of Yoga scholar Ernest Wood, who translates this principle of Ishvara Pranidhana as 'Attentiveness to God,' which Wood defines as "the acceptance of all experience without resentment or antagonism, not merely seeing the good in everything, but seeing the God in everything, which puts our emotions as well as our understanding right." [45]

As Wood suggests, this principle guides you to allow human feelings to simply be present, access inner knowledge, and listen to your innate guidance. It is about reaching for the Divine wisdom within you and the highest vibrations of your Spirit or soul. This can be done in the reverence of silent meditation, in a Yoga session, on a peaceful boat ride, on a walk in nature, in the bathtub, or in any prayerful experience that calls to you. Perhaps we can call this principle of Ishvara Pranidhana-- the practice of taking time from our daily concerns and self-attention to focus on connecting with the Divine Source of the Universe. Nothing is surrendered and a wider perspective is gained!

Prayer is the greatest way to practice "Attentiveness to God" and access your inner Divinity with gratitude. It is your pathway to the Higher Powers of the Universe and the Oneness of all.

---

[45] Wood, Ernest, *Yoga* (Maryland: Penguin Books, 1961), p. 44.

As mentioned in the previous chapter, I have learned that the best prayer is an affirmative prayer that thanks the Divine Universe in advance for fulfilling my needs and desires. It is wise to avoid woeful, lamenting prayers that focus on the scarcity of what you are praying for. Here, I invite you to remember our first chapter about dropping into your heart and feeling the comfort of knowing that your prayers are being heard and answered.

Prayers come from the heart (not mental treatises), calling you to feel the Presence of a Higher Power more deeply and express genuine gratitude, love, and appreciation for life's gifts and the gift of life itself. "Feeling" that your prayer is being answered is the key to manifesting the greater good you seek.

Sharing My Personal Prayer Walk Practices

"Begin to live as though your prayers are already answered."

--*Tony* Robbins, Motivational Speaker and Author

As I scribbled down the middle-of-the-night messages I received about accessing a deeper spiritual connection to all of life, I realized that this is what I do daily as I commune with nature on my solo hikes out in the red rocks. Before I share my personal prayer walk practice, I would like to put it in context. When the pandemic first hit, and we were all shut in, I missed the hiking I did with clients. So, I started to go out by myself to the empty Red Rock State Park, one of the few scenic spots that was open to the public, to just be out among the red rocks and feel the healing energy that nature provides.

The fear, loss, and sorrow that the pandemic brought prompted me to say all of the prayers I ever knew, not just for my family, friends, and clients, but for humanity and the earth. Now, a few of years later, I still love going out for my morning prayer walk and connecting with the Universe.

Every day I can, I go out for my prayer walk amid the red rocks of Sedona. It helps lift my spirits to connect with the magnificence of nature and the goodness of the Universe and to feel gratitude for the many blessings in my life. This walk, usually at Red Rock State Park, connects me with my soul's highest good for at least the entire day, no matter what the current life circumstances may be.

While my heart prays, my eyes appreciate all of nature as I pass juniper trees, prickly pear cacti, manzanita bushes, and magnificent red rocks leading to the Cathedral Rock Vortex overlook. I am fully present with Mother Earth as prayers flow from my heart. Let me briefly share the collection of different prayers that I have learned over a lifetime of 70+ years and how they strengthen me.

Catholic Prayers

First, as I walk over a stately wooden bridge beneath giant Cottonwood trees, I scan the grass by the creek for deer and look in the creek for the frequently present ducks and a mud turtle I have named Marty. I begin by blessing myself with the sign of the cross and saying the Catholic prayers that have taught me to connect with God since childhood. I have changed the words a bit, deleting any reference to being a sinner, but I truly feel that saying the *Our Father, Hail Mary,* and *Glory Be* prayers helps me expand my consciousness as I pray for the people in my life and everyone on earth.

Tree Hugging

After slowly crossing the bridge, I hug the flourishing giant Cottonwood tree called the Wedding Tree, estimated to be 150 years old. I thank God for the blessings of this tree that inspires me to be like it—rooted in the earth, standing tall and healthy, enjoying longevity, reaching into the heavens, flourishing. As I hug this tree with my upper torso pressed against it, I ask it to fill my heart and solar plexus with strength.

Smiling, I leave my blessed tree filled with grace and walk towards the hill leading to the scenic Cathedral Rock Vortex overlook. I was recently happy to hear from an arborist that this Cottonwood tree knows me and is hugging me back.

5-Step Spiritual Mind Treatment

My prayer walk continues as I recite a favorite affirmation— *"There is one life. That life is good. That life is God. That life is perfect. That life is my life now."*

That is how I always begin Ernest Holmes' five-part spiritual mind treatment that I learned from my dear teacher Reverend Christian Sorensen at the Seaside Center for Spiritual Living in California.

I say all five parts, feeling them in my heart: 1- I recognize that God pervades all of existence; 2- I acknowledge that all creatures are one; 3-I thank God for fulfilling the needs and desires affirmed in my prayer today; 4- I express gratitude for the abundant blessings already in my life; and 5- I powerfully launch my heartfelt gratitude, thanking God for watching over me, fulfilling my desires, and answering today's prayer for myself and others. I end this heart-warming visit with God, feeling that my prayers have already been heard and answered.

Energy Exchange with Cathedral Rock Vortex

Then, as I slowly climb the steep red rock path to reach the top of the hill, I view the magnificent spires of Cathedral Rock Vortex and take time to commune with its cleansing energy. I raise my arms up and create a circle of energy between us, as I let go of anything that I want to release through my legs and feet into the earth. My arms scoop up the energy of this magnificent Cathedral Rock and bring it into my heart and being. I place my hands with fingers spread and thumbs hooked across my chest, in a Yoga heart mudra (hand gesture), feeling nurtured by this feminine vortex and one with Mother Earth.

Before leaving the majesty of Cathedral Rock, I lift my arms above my head to open my eighth chakra, my *Wiracocha* or soul essence, calling upon the Universe to create sacred space for my Shamanic medicine wheel prayer.

Shamanic Prayer to the Four Directions

As I turn around and walk past the House of Apache Fires, I bless all the people who created it and those who continue to maintain this magnificent house on the sacred hill. I move on to saying my Shamanic prayer to the Four Directions, the Lords of the Three Worlds, Mother Earth, and Father Sky. I say my personal rendition of the Inca medicine wheel prayer that I learned in Alberto Villoldo's Four Winds Shamanic Energy Medicine Training.[46]

In the Peruvian tradition of the Shamans, I thank the Four Directions and Keepers of Three Worlds for their magnificent guidance and continued blessings, not in a manner of worship but in gratitude for what they symbolically represent. In this Shamanic medicine wheel prayer,

[46] http://www.thefourwinds.com

I first thank the South and *Sacha Mama*, the Serpent—for inspiring me to let go of any negativity (giving specifics about current difficulties) the way she sheds her skin and glides around obstacles hugging the earth, as the Shamans say, in "the beauty way."

Second, I thank the West and *Otorongo*, Sister Jaguar—for giving me the strength and courage to deal with my thoughts and emotions (taking the time to name and feel them) and express my gratitude for the tracking prowess the Jaguar inspires to help me to stay in dominion of my life.

Third, I go on to thank the North, *Sirakinti*, the Hummingbird and all of my Ancestors—for their guidance and blessings. I thank them for teaching me stillness in motion and inspiring me to take all of life's experiences to a higher spiritual plane and taste joy and abundance everywhere.

Fourth, I thank the East and *Apuchin,* the Eagle—for helping me rise above my human challenges and soar to the mountaintops, connecting me with the highest Divine Energy. From this mountaintop, I look down on my little human life which seems very tiny and insignificant in comparison to the vast Divine Consciousness that I am.

Thanking the East for the sunrise that brings me this new day, I let go of all concerns and trust that a Divine Universe is looking after me. I affirm "I am that I am." And I love to whisper to myself—"God's got my back."

Continuing my prayer in the tradition of Peruvian Shamans, I thank the Keepers of the Three Worlds for their magnificent guidance and continued blessings, thinking about what they symbolically represent. I say a prayer thanking *Huascar*, the Lord of the Underworld, for helping me release subconscious fears and heal on an unconscious level.

I express gratitude to *Quetzalcoatl*, the Lord of the Middle World, for guiding my conscious steps each day to be in "right relationship" (as the Shamans would say) with everyone and everything in my everyday life, citing the most recent guidance I am thankful for today.

And I thank *Pachakuti*, the Lord of Higher Consciousness, for blessing me with expanded consciousness and calling me forth on a superconscious level to develop my inner goodness, love, and Light. I give thanks for being able to contribute my best in all relationships, teaching, coaching, and writing in union with Spirit.

Lastly, I thank Mother Earth and the Sea and Father Sun and the Sky, all creatures and heavenly beings, for their blessings and healing energy. I end my beautiful, bolstering Shamanic medicine ceremony by reverently closing sacred space and drawing in my *Wiracocha,* or inner soul essence, that I called upon to bless my prayer.

Feeling cleansed and deeply connected, I continue meandering on my path, appreciating the landscapes and red rock views, enjoying the silence as I feel truly connected to the vastness of the Universe. Lastly, my prayer turns to Sanskrit mantras.

Sanskrit Mantras

Proceeding across winding trails on Coyote Ridge, I pause at a Juniper tree under which I placed a heart shaped rock during a ceremony I led for two honeymooners. I take a moment to bless them and all of my Sedona Spirit Yoga guests—present, past, and future. Turning down the hill on a winding trail to the bridge below, I marvel at the side view of the House of Apache Fires with Cathedral Rock behind it, feeling gratitude for this new day as my feet start to scamper down the trail. Moving quickly, I repeat wonderful Sanskrit mantras that I learned from my blessed Amma and Deepak Chopra, feeling that I am receiving their blessings within my heart. My favorites are the personal mantra that Amma gave me and seven sutra statements from the Deepak Chopra book that I mentioned earlier, ***The Spontaneous Fulfillment of Desire.***

To give you an example, the first and paramount sutra statement Chopra shares is "*Aham Brahmasmi (ah-HUM-brahMAHS-mee)*," which he defines as "The core of my being is the ultimate reality, the root, and ground of the Universe, the source of all that exists." [47] The second sutra statement is "*Tat Tvam Asi (taht t'vahm AH-see)*," which Deepak Chopra defines as "I see the other in myself and myself in others." [48]

Repeating these mantras helps me feel that I am part of the Source of all life and that the core of my being is connected to the core of all beings. If you are as intrigued by these mantras as I am, perhaps you will enjoy learning Chopra's sutra statement for each day of the week. I have memorized the Sanskrit and English translations of all seven and enjoy saying them multiple times each day, feeling the expanded connection they bring.

Approaching the exit bridge as I prepare to leave Red Rock State Park, I look around at nature encircling me and bid farewell, thanking all of the trees, plants, and red rocks for this invigorating experience. I look in each direction, bidding a grateful farewell to the House of Apache Fires up the hill and to the Wedding Tree across from the bridge.

Once again, I look into the creek water to see if I can find Marty, my mud turtle, but I think he has moved on. As I cross the bridge to exit the park, I sometimes take photos of white-bottomed mule deer in the meadow, hummingbirds in the garden, or the vibrant hot pink lotus flowers floating in the pond outside the Visitor Center.

Finally, I arrive at my car feeling buoyant and blessed, ready to greet whatever the day might bring. Being out in nature and taking time to commune with landscapes, streams, trees, birds, and animals is a great way to connect with life.

---

[47] Chopra, Deepak, *The Essential Spontaneous Fulfillment of Desire: The Essence of Harnessing the Infinite Power of Coincidence* (New York: Harmony Books, 2003), p. 181.

[48] Chopra, Deepak, *The Essential Spontaneous Fulfillment of Desire: The Essence of Harnessing the Infinite Power of Coincidence* (New York: Harmony Books, 2003), p. 186.

And my time with my Higher Self and expanded consciousness does not end there. Throughout the day's myriad activities, I stay connected to Spirit, my inner essence, and the Invisible Energy pervading life. My business, Sedona Spirit Yoga, gives me the privilege of connecting with people on a spiritual level. I help them do their *Soul Stretch* with coaching, Yoga, meditation, and Shamanic energy clearing—whether on the phone, via email, red rock vortex journeys, indoor private sessions, or retreats. At night, when I settle into bed, my prayer continues to lull me into sleep as I thank the Universe for the particular blessings of the day, the clients who came, the friends who called, the writing I did, and the strength to handle anything that did not seem to go well. Now that I have told clients about my prayer vigil, they are eager to follow in my footsteps.

It's Not HOW You Pray, Just THAT You Pray. Do It Your Way!

As you can see, my practice is an eclectic collection of traditions from different cultures and religions, prayers calling upon the blessings of the Universe that I learned from childhood and have carried throughout my life and studies. Please understand that you are NOT expected to replicate MY prayer walk, but you are invited to design your own, no matter how simple or complex it may be.

It's not about HOW you pray. It's about reaching into the vastness beyond the smallness of your personal world. How can you cultivate your highest self and expand your consciousness to connect with the Mysterious Energies orchestrating your life?

Your prayer might be the silence of meditation, without words or even a drop-into-the-heart moment, as I wrote about in a preceding chapter. For you, it might be Yoga, taking a nature walk, going fishing, babysitting a newborn grandchild, or visiting a favorite temple or church.

Let's not forget the pathway to Higher Consciousness that religions provide. The three basic *Soul Stretch* prayer ingredients are deep feeling, gratitude, and belief in a Divine Energy that hears and answers your prayers. The principle of surrendering to a Higher Force is based on believing in a bigger picture than your little life's scenario. It entails trusting that the more you focus on believing that a Divine Intelligence is caring for and providing for you, the more you can see it and feel it blessing your life.

What Is Your Mind's Computer Downloading?

"At all costs we must re-establish faith in spiritual values.

We must worship something beyond ourselves,

lest we destroy ourselves."

– Sir Philip Gibbs, English Journalist and Novelist

What is your mind's computer downloading? Does it need to be rebooted regularly? It is beyond just recharging batteries. It's about staying "plugged in" to your Higher Self, *trusting your inner guidance and reaching high* to summon the best that you personally have to offer.

It's about staying connected and receiving the blessings that surround you when you are present to download them. It's about being a clear channel for life's goodness to flow through you.

As you can now see, this principle of Surrendering to God helps you to nurture your spiritual connection with your higher self, with other beings, and with the entire Field of Invisible Consciousness. It is your connection to the deepest goodness that life has to offer. Practicing this kind of "attentiveness to God" is a way to have your ego step aside and make way for your true life purpose to reveal itself. Stay plugged in and *reach high*!

Benefits of Surrendering to a Higher Power

"Ishvara Pranidhana will help to cure the afflictions of the mind that cause pain and suffering, as it is designed to redirect our energy away from out selfish desires and personal dramas and towards the ultimate pursuit of Oneness." [49]

The Yoga Sutras claim that you can transcend the suffering of the human condition by surrendering and accepting the flow of events. By surrendering your ego's personal desires to the Intelligence of the Universe, you learn to perform actions for their own sake without attachment to outcomes, realizing that there is a flow to what happens in life and a Force that guides it.

You feel connected with all that is and understand that you are a small, individualized part of a giant Universal Field of Consciousness. In offering whatever you do for the well-being of the whole, you find peace in knowing that things will happen as they are meant to.

The sutras suggest that the rewards for surrendering to a Higher Power can be a heightened awareness of the vast blessings of being alive and a joyous sense of Oneness with all of life. Surrendering with faith and trust can lead to a sublime union with internal and external Goodness, God, your chosen deity, Mother Nature, or whatever you believe to be the Divine Source orchestrating the Universe. Such surrender can lead to supreme bliss.

---

[49] http://www.jivamuktiyoga.com

This principle *Ishvara Pranidhana* teaches you to live in gratitude and grace, offering whatever you do to the Highest Good with all your heart and soul. Reaching into the deepest connection with all that is, your *soul stretches* into cultivating the best you, nurturing the highest consciousness you have to personally enjoy and share with others.

Everyday Examples of Lack of Surrender

Here are several everyday examples of the need to let go of trying to control life and surrender outcomes to a Higher Power. Which ones might you relate to?

- Getting upset if others don't agree
- Feeling broken-hearted if your plan fails
- Becoming distressed if your expectations are not met
- Repeatedly pushing for something that's not happening
- Blaming yourself or others when you don't get results
- Insisting on taking action when logistics are not falling into place
- Thinking you should have done something to prevent an incident
- Feeling personally responsible for everything that goes wrong
- Being more focused on personal success than on contributing
- Forgetting that you are not orchestrating the bigger picture

Discussion and Journaling on Surrender to a Higher Power -- Good Notices, Ahas, Gratitude, Fun Scribbling, Intentions, Shifts, and Self-Care

- What are your thoughts about Surrendering to a Higher Power?
- To what extent do you feel that the results of your actions are in the hands of a Higher Power?
- Are there any past occasions in which you faced challenges trying to control people and events?
- Can you recall what happened a time you surrendered your desired outcomes to welcome life's flow?
- In what ways and at what times do you feel connected to a Higher Source?
- Can you think of new ways you might let go of personal striving and trust the flow of life more fully?

Ways to Surrender into Ishvara-Pranidhana

To deepen my inner connection with the Source of the Universe, I will take the following steps:

- I will be mindful to surrender my ego when I am intent on having my way with people, projects, and activities. I will broaden my perspective to think of others.
- I will do my best to expand my consciousness from shortsighted self-importance to a larger world view and find ways to contribute my best to the highest good for all.

- I will accept situations that do not go well for me and stay centered with "Attentiveness" to a Higher Power. I will plant seeds for change and trust that the Universe will provide abundance for me when the time is right.

Now that you have looked into your deepest connection with Spirit, you have come home to your Divine Being.

Affirmations

- I see the goodness in all beings
- I am one with the whole Universe
- I am filled with Divine Light
- I surrender the illusion of control
- I embrace prayerful connection
- Thy will not mine be done

"Drop In" for Surrender to a Higher Power

- Sit in a quiet place and close your eyes
- Breathe into feeling the love in your heart
- Label exterior sensations and let them go
- Nestle into a peaceful, loving place within
- Appreciate yourself for trusting that you are guided by a Higher Power
- Thank the Universe for the goodness of life

Taking It All Home

Now that we have had a chance to explore the ten *Sedona Soul Stretch* principles to expand Consciousness, let's look at how to bring it all home. Allow me to do an impressionistic rendering of your journey thus far by summarizing the five **Characteristics of Social Harmony** and the five **Codes for Soulful Living**. Then we will look at ways to incorporate these precepts into your daily life. How can you live each day with a deeper connection to your spiritual essence and the vast Energy Field surrounding you?

Five Social Harmony Principles for Success and Well-Being

Let's review the five **Social Harmony Principles:** highlighting **Compassion, Truthfulness, Non-Stealing, Moderation,** and **Non-Attachment**. The first idea is to ***Stay Centered in Your Heart*** and always be Compassionate to yourself and others. Living from your heart, you care how your thoughts, words, and actions affect everyone. You make it a priority to treat all living creatures with kindness and reverence.

By remaining heart-centered, you ***Stay Aligned*** with the Truth of who you are. Being your authentic self, you are gentle, honest, and forthright. In all your endeavors, you remain aligned with the right thought, speech, and action, being true to yourself and everyone you meet.

You ***Keep Your Eyes on Your Own Mat*** while honoring yourself and others. You respect what belongs to them without coveting, jealousy, or theft. You create healthy boundaries, cultivate your best life, and refrain from taking anything that is not freely offered to you.

By wisely choosing Moderation, you ***Do Not Stretch Too Far*** or allow any excesses to deplete your energy. You take care to be temperate as you pursue pleasurable experiences. You curb the tendency to overdo anything, be it eating, drinking, watching media, socializing, worrying, or burning the midnight oil to meet a deadline.

By learning to ***Relax Your Grip*** on people, projects, and possessions, you practice Non-Attachment. You do your best to surrender the desire to control relationships, events, and outcomes in your life. Always promoting the welfare of others as well as your own, you expand beyond your concern with "Me, My, I" and broaden your focus to serve everyone's highest good.

By practicing these five essential human traits, you can enjoy what the Peruvian Shamans call "right relationship" with yourself and the rest of humanity. You are mindful to live authentically, true to your own self, while compassionately caring for all creatures. You develop healthy boundaries, respecting what belongs to others, without clinging or succumbing to extremes. You flourish when you keep high positive energy by being kind, telling the truth, being moderate, not stealing, and refraining from attachment.

Five Principles for Soulful Living and Personal Mastery

As you can see, it's important to have the right relationship with the outer world to achieve harmony and success with family, friends, colleagues, and companions. You have also seen that the second set of five **Codes for Soulful Living—Purity, Contentment, Discipline, Self-Study,** and **Surrender to a Higher Power**—guides you to focus on your personal development and the connection between your consciousness and the Universal Intelligence Field.

As we have discussed, the first essential step toward self- mastery is to ***Stay Clean and Focused*** inside your head and heart and outside with others and your environment. You try to keep things clean, see clearly, tap into your inner knowing, and avoid confusing distractions, roller-coaster emotions, and hidden agendas.

You learn to ***Smile into Each Stretch*** that life's ups and downs offer by developing inner clarity and cultivating Contentment. You remember that it's your job to accept whatever happens and not let it throw you off-center. And if it does disturb your equilibrium, you adjust as quickly as possible to regain a sense of balance. You become okay with whatever happens, at least for the time being, while you take steps to create more desirable outcomes.

You summon the Discipline to remain satisfied with life when difficulties occur. You ***Hold the Pose Through Challenges***, aiming to change whatever you can for the better, accepting what you cannot change, and trusting the rest to the Universe. You maintain the Discipline to veer away from distractions and stay focused on achieving your goals for the highest good.

Learning to Discipline your thoughts, words, and actions brings you to the practice of Self-Study. To heighten your performance and your enjoyment of life, you learn to ***Reflect on Your Practice***, remaining mindful and frequently asking, "How am I doing?" You think about the effect of the many decisions you make each day—your thoughts, words, actions, and your choice of activities, companions, and indulgences. When you practice Self-Study, you raise your awareness of your daily behaviors and consider whether there are any changes that might help you improve, always without any self-blame..

And this brings you to our pinnacle of principles, ***Surrender to a Higher Power***. You continue to develop a strong relationship between your soul and the Powers of the Universe. You learn to tap into and trust both the Energy Field around you and your inner guidance. You make sure to uplift your Spirit and feel connected to your soul through prayer, meditation, Yoga, reflective journal writing, communing with nature, or anything else that brings you joy and serenity. By remaining connected to your spiritual essence, you can experience Oneness with all of life, achieve peace of mind, and discover your true purpose for being alive.

You Can Apply these Ancient Principles to Expand Your Consciousness Today

Here are a few suggestions to help you keep these principles at the forefront of your mind and heart--

- **Make a List of the Ten Yoga Principles**—Keep the list visible in your cell phone notes, on your computer's desktop, on your bedside nightstand, on your bathroom mirror, your refrigerator door, or in your car's glove compartment.
- **Keep a Journal Notebook**—Write a list of the ten principles on the first page, and keep journal entries about how well you are living these codes for well-being and the shifts you intend to make. Always remember to to refrain from any blame and congratulate yourself, saying "Good Notice!"

- **Start a Yoga Principles Discussion Group**—Share these concepts at a community gathering, a book club, a support group, a business meeting, or a family gathering, discussing the nature of the principles and how they relate to events in the lives of those present.
- **Share the Yoga Principles with a Partner**—Choose someone you speak to regularly who would like to be your Yoga Principles Partner, and make a commitment for each of you to live these precepts and share their effect on your daily lives.
- **Reflect on the Yoga Principles at Bedtime**—As my teacher, the departed Georg Feuerstein, practiced in his own life, you might review at bedtime how well you lived the principles each day and then set an intention to live them more fully the next day.

Imagine What It Would FEEL Like...

- To live centered in your heart more than in your head
- To be fully at peace with yourself and your life no matter what happens
- To know you are truly connected to the Mysterious Energy orchestrating the Universe
- To see people everywhere embracing integrity and honoring boundaries
- To trust that the Divine Consciousness is really hearing your prayers and answering them to know that you are fulfilling your life's purpose for the highest good

Imagine What It Would BE Like...

- To drop negative thinking and actions and be kinder to yourself and others
- To reflect on things you would like to shift and say "Good Notice" instead of assigning blame
- To feel the Oneness of all people and a kindred connection with everyone, even those unlike you
- To truly get to know and trust your Higher Self to make the right decisions for you
- To believe that each day is a gift of grace for your soul to stretch into
- To see everyone on earth living these ten ancient principles with caring hearts and reverence for all life

It's all possible, one *Soul Stretch* at a time. I invite you to join me in embracing these ten ancient principles as your way of life. I leave you with my Divine Love and Blessings and the wise words of Maya Angelou as I hold each of you in my heart and prayers.

"This is a wonderful day,
I have never seen this one before."

Sedona Soul Stretch Bibliography

- Blanchard, Ken and Hutson, Don with Willis, Ethan. The One Minute Entrepreneur. Pennsylvania: Executive Books, 2007.
- Covert, Jack and Sattersten, Todd. The 100 Best Business Books of All Time: What They Say, Why They Matter, and How They Can Help You. New York: Penguin Group, 2009.
- Carnegie, Dale. How to Win Friends & Influence People. New York: Simon and Schuster, 1936.
- Chopra, Deepak. The Spontaneous Fulfillment of Desire: Harnessing the Infinite Power of Coincidence. New York: Harmony Books, 2003.
- Covey Stephen R. Principle-Centered Leadership. New York: Simon and Schuster, 1990.
- Covey, Stephen R. The 7 Habits of Highly Effective People: Restoring the Character Ethic. New York: Simon and Schuster, 1989.
- Desikachar, T.K.V. with Cravens, R.H. Health, Healing and Beyond: Yoga and the Living Tradition of Krishnamacharya. New York: Aperture Foundation, Inc., 1998.
- Desikachar, T.K.V. Reflections on Yoga Sutras of Patanjali. India: Krishnamacharya Yoga Mandarim, 1987.
- Drucker, Peter F. The Effective Executive: The Definitive Guide to Getting it Right. New York: Harper Collins Publishers, 1996.
- Farhi, Donna. Yoga, Mind, Body and Spirit: A Return to Wholeness. Texas: Holt Mc Dougal, 2000.

- Ghandi, Arun. Legacy of Love: My Education on the Path of Nonviolence. California: Berkeley Hills Books, 2001.
- Hari Dass, Baba, edited by Ault, Karuna K., and illustrated by Jones, Steven. The Ashtanga Primer. India: Sri Rama Publishing, 1981 and second edition 2019.
- Hill, Napoleon. Success Habits: Proven Principles for Greater Wealth, Health, and Happiness. New York: St. Martin's Press, 2018.
- Hill, Napoleon. Think and Grow Rich. New York: Ballantine Books, Random House, 1963.
- Iyengar, B.K.S. Light on Yoga. New York: Shocken Books, 1966.
- Iyengar, B.K.S. Light on the Yoga Sutras of Patanjali. California: Harper Collins, 1996.
- Kofman, Fred. Conscious Business: How to Build Value Through Values. Colorado: Sounds True, 2006.
- Lipton, Bruce H. The Biology of Belief: Unleashing the Power of Consciousness, Matter and Miracles. California: Hay House, 2008.
- Mirdad, Michael. Healing the Heart and Soul. Arizona: Grail Productions, Inc., 2011.
- Mosca, Johanna. Cultivate Contentment: Using Ancient Wisdom to Thrive in Today's World. Arizona: Sedona Spirit Yoga Publications, 2009.
- Mosca, Johanna. YogaLife: 10 Steps to Freedom. Arizona: Sedona Spirit Yoga Publications, 2000.
- Rath, Tom and Clifton, Donald. How Full is Your Bucket? Positive Strategies for Work and Life. New York: Gallup Press, 2004.
- Robbins, Tony. Unlimited Power: The New Science of Personal Achievement. New York: Free Press, Simon and Schuster, 1997.
- Ruiz, Don Miguel. The Four Agreements: A Practical guide to Personal Freedom. California: Amber-Allen Publishing, 1997

- Ruiz, Don Miguel and Ruiz, Don Jose. The Fifth Agreement: A Practical Guide to Self-Mastery. California: Amber-Allen Publishing, 2010.
- Satchidananda, Sri Swami. The Yoga Sutras of Patanjali. Virginia: Integral Yoga Publications, 1978.
- Shearer, Alistair. The Yoga Sutras of Patanjali. New York: Bell Tower, 1982.
- Slap, Stan. Under the Hood: Fire Up and Fine Tune Your Employee Culture New York: Penguin Group, 2015.
- Tang, Connie. Fearless Living: 8 Life-Changing Values for Breakthrough Success. Tennessee: Clovercroft Publishing, 2017.
- Virtue, Doreen. Chakra Clearing: Awakening your Spiritual Power to Know and Heal. California: Hay House, Inc., 1998, second edition 2004.
- Villoldo, Alberto. Yoga, Power, and Spirit: Patanjali the Shaman. California: Hay House, 2007.
- Yogananda, Paramahansa. Where there is Light. California: Self-Realization Fellowship, 1988.

www.ingramcontent.com/pod-product-compliance
Lightning Source LLC
Chambersburg PA
CBHW070914130626
46555CB00001B/135

9798988540007